MINISTRY OF PRESENCE

Biblical Insight on Christian Chaplaincy

Whit Woodard, M. Div, D. Min

Faithful Life Publishers
North Fort Myers, FL
FaithfulLifePublishers.com

ISBN: 978-0-9832039-2-6

Published, printed and distributed by:
Faithful Life Publishers
3335 Galaxy Way
North Fort Myers, FL   33903

www.FaithfulLifePublishers.com

info@FLPublishers,com

Printed in the United States of America
19 18 17 16 15 14 13 12 11   1 2 3 4 5

For over a decade, Chaplain Whit Woodard and I have worked together to advance military chaplaincy. Whit's book is the result of deep gratitude for the privilege of call to minister as a chaplain. He couples this with sober concern that chaplains and chaplaincies will serve the spiritual welfare of the Troops in the best possible fashion. Whit is clear about his particular theological perspective from cover to cover. It was a distinct pleasure to engage with and even debate some of his arguments within such integrity of biblical and theological framework. Whit's material has virtue and implications well beyond the ministry specialty of military chaplaincy. His text would be quite valuable on the reading list of general courses in ecclesiology and pastoral theology.

> Rev. Dr. Gary R. Pollitt, Ph.D.
> Captain, CHC, U. S. Navy (Ret)
> Executive Director
> Military Chaplains Association

MINISTRY OF PRESENCE speaks to the heart of chaplaincy. It deals with the history and definition of chaplaincy, the chaplain's call to ministry, and relationship to his church. Specific concerns such as pluralism, prayer, and proselytizing are also addressed. MINISTRY OF PRESENCE is a resource for those already in the chaplaincy, chaplain candidates, or anyone interested in learning about chaplaincy. The principles presented are not simply theory but are born out of the context of Woodard's experience and practicing what he preaches. His insights will encourage and challenge anyone seeking to minister from a biblical perspective in any venue of ministry.

> Dr. John B. Murdoch
> Director of Chaplaincy Ministry
> General Association of Regular Baptist Churches
>
> Chaplain, Colonel, CAP
> Chief of Chaplains Emeritus
> United States Air Force Auxiliary, Civil Air Patrol

QUOTES TAKEN FROM THE BOOK

"Chaplaincy deals with life where the rubber meets the road."

"A chaplain who lacks a solid grounding in the Word of God and biblical theology is likely to be drawn away from the truth by the socially attractive fiction of the world, and even unwittingly encourage a misleading gospel that denigrates the sovereignty of God."

"It is not always necessary to have experienced the same tribulation or trouble to avail oneself of the same comfort of God, but there certainly is an implication that the one who is called upon to comfort is likely to endure affliction of some sort in preparation for such a ministry."

"...it is clear that there must also be some objective measure of qualification that encompasses the biblical admonition for godliness and the practical challenges of ministry."

"How then does one determine whether his desire to enter a vocational (divinely appointed) ministry is a genuine call of God?"

"The most crucial problem facing chaplaincy today is the failure to engage the local church in the oversight of chaplains."

"The pressing question that must be answered is whether pluralism prevents a bible-believing Christian minister from performing the duties of a chaplain without compromising his doctrinal beliefs."

"There is a biblical strategy for ministry in a pluralistic culture."

"The burning question facing Christian chaplains is this: Must a Christian recite the words "in Jesus' name" (or a reasonable facsimile) for a prayer to be biblically acceptable?"

"Christian chaplains need not be intimidated by concerns about proselytizing..."

Table of Contents

INTRODUCTION

Many years ago as a very new Christian and before I entertained any thoughts of ministry I heard the story of a British cleric who had visited the United States. Upon his return, he was asked how he would define religion in America to which he responded by saying: "Grape Nuts and Christian Science." Bewildered by such a cryptic answer, his protégés pressed him for an explanation. I have long since forgotten what year he visited our shores, but I shall never forget his description. He said: "In America they have a cereal called Grape Nuts that is neither grapes nor nuts; and they have a religion called Christian Science that is neither Christian nor scientific."

There are two defining words that must be truly applied to this writing if it is to accomplish its purpose. They are "Christian" and "biblical," and for some, I am sure, they will place a perceived limitation on its value. Fully understanding that chaplaincy comprises many religions and philosophies, I choose to focus my thoughts on *Christian* chaplaincy. There is no denying that many compassionate and dedicated souls who do not embrace a Christian world view engage in chaplain service of one sort or another, and even accomplish much that is good. I respect their honest and honorable intentions and commend their commitment to helping others. I have served beside them in the throes of trauma and crisis. No doubt they are sincerely attempting to fulfill the desire expressed by our Lord Jesus that we love our neighbor, but I have no opinion or authority to offer them apart from the Word of God, and the good news that the Lord Jesus Christ died a voluntary and propitiatory death for their sins as He did for mine.

That brings me to the second descriptor – *biblical*. This is to be a biblical perspective and not a societal one, though it would be impossible and irresponsible to overlook the influence of society on chaplaincy, and certainly unwise not to address how Christians ought to deal with that influence. Be that as it may, I am not attracted so much by cultural influences, as by direction from God's Holy Word. I believe with all my heart the inspired words of the Apostle Paul recorded in 2 Timothy 3:16, 17: "All Scripture is breathed out by God and profitable for teaching, for reproof, for correction, and for training in righteousness, that the man of God may be competent, equipped for every good work."

This discussion is offered in the hope that the reader will epitomize the spirit of the Bereans of old of whom it is recorded in Acts 17:11 "...they received the word with all eagerness, examining the Scriptures daily to see if these things were so."

CHAPTER ONE

CHAPLAINCY DEFINED

As we drove through the parking lot behind a somewhat infamous motel on the edge of town, a man and two women nervously glanced over their shoulders at the approach of the police car. They appeared to be interested in some trash beside the dumpster. When questioned by the officer, they said that they were just looking for cans and bottles and were staying the night in the motel. Something about them just didn't ring true as the officer radioed in for a records check. One of the girls was on probation and it was apparent she had been drinking. The officer took her aside for questioning and motioned for the man and his other companion to stand by the police car. He quietly said to me, "Keep an eye on them, Chaplain." Not an unusual request. I had done so many times before. Taking a position where I could watch the "suspects" and the officer, I studied my charges carefully. Several questions entered my mind. What would we learn about them? Would they attempt to run if derogatory information was revealed? Would they place me or the officer in danger? Their body language made me wonder if they had been taking drugs. I watched carefully to make sure they didn't produce some sort of weapon, politely, but firmly insisting they keep their hands out of their pockets. They, too, studied me, no doubt sizing me up as well. The man took in my uniform with gold crosses on my collar. He noted my badge clearly emblazoned with the word "CHAPLAIN." Finally, he blurted out: "What is a Chaplain?"

Not an unusual question. I had been asked the same many times before in similar circumstances. At first it seemed strange that anyone would ask such a question. It had always seemed pretty self-evident to me, but many years as a law enforcement chaplain had taught me that what may be common knowledge to the "churched," is often a foreign concept to the "un-churched." Come to think of it, that question might be profitably asked by many who have attended Christian churches for years. What IS a chaplain?

A chaplain is not a pastor, because he is not charged with the leadership of a local church. Though chaplains are often pastors as well, they have distinctly different skill sets. They have a shared calling, but differing responsibilities that may coincidentally engage the same individual. The New Testament makes it clear that a pastor is a gift to the Church with the specific purpose of perfecting believers for the work of the ministry. Writing to the church in Ephesus, Paul revealed a foundational principle of pastoral leadership:

> [11] And he gave some, apostles; and some, prophets; and some, evangelists; and some, pastors and teachers; [12] For the perfecting of the saints, for the work of the ministry, for the edifying of the body of Christ: [13] Till we all come in the unity of the faith, and of the knowledge of the Son of God, unto a perfect man, unto the measure of the stature of the fullness of Christ: [14] That we *henceforth* be no more children, tossed to and fro, and carried about with every wind of doctrine, by the sleight of men, *and* cunning craftiness, whereby they lie in wait to deceive;" Ephesians 4:10–14 KJV

Paul was acutely aware of the danger to believers who were confronted by the efforts of those who prey on the sheep. He warned Pastor Timothy, who was charged with the leadership of the church in Ephesus, of false teachers who were "desiring to be teachers…, without understanding either what they are saying or the things about which they make confident assertions."[1] In

---

1   1 Timothy 1:7

God's economy, pastors are employed to see to the perfection [maturation] of believers lest they be tossed about by the cunning deceptions that blow about them.

By the direction of the Holy Spirit, Paul went on to remind Pastor Timothy that some would depart from the faith and give way to seducing spirits and doctrines of devils, speaking lies with a seared conscience. "Now the Spirit expressly says that in later times some will depart from the faith by devoting themselves to deceitful spirits and teachings of demons, through the insincerity of liars whose consciences are seared,..."[2] He sums up that challenge by admonishing Timothy to "put these things before the brothers," and if he does so, he will "be a good servant of Christ Jesus, being trained in the words of the faith and of the good doctrine that [he] ... followed."[3]

Pastors are charged with many tasks, and principal among them is the doctrinal leadership of the church. This is made plain in the authority given to the pastor who is not only described in scripture as a shepherd and an elder, but also as a bishop.

[17] Now from Miletus he sent to Ephesus and called the **elders** of the church to come to him. [18] And when they came to him, he said to them: "You yourselves know how I lived among you the whole time from the first day that I set foot in Asia, [19] serving the Lord with all humility and with tears and with trials that happened to me through the plots of the Jews; [20] how I did not shrink from declaring to you anything that was profitable, and teaching you in public and from house to house, [21] testifying both to Jews and to Greeks of repentance toward God and of faith in our Lord Jesus Christ. [22] And now, behold, I am going to Jerusalem, constrained by the Spirit, not knowing what will happen to me there, [23] except that the Holy Spirit testifies to me in every city that imprisonment

2   1 Timothy 4: 1, 2
3   1 Timothy 4:6

and afflictions await me. ²⁴ But I do not account my life of any value nor as precious to myself, if only I may finish my course and the ministry that I received from the Lord Jesus, to testify to the gospel of the grace of God. ²⁵ And now, behold, I know that none of you among whom I have gone about proclaiming the kingdom will see my face again. ²⁶ Therefore I testify to you this day that I am innocent of the blood of all of you, ²⁷ for I did not shrink from declaring to you the whole counsel of God. ²⁸ Pay careful attention to yourselves and to all the flock, in which the Holy Spirit has made you **overseers,** to **care for** the church of God, which he obtained with his own blood. ²⁹ I know that after my departure fierce wolves will come in among you, not sparing the flock..." Acts 20:17–29 (Emphasis mine)

The word *overseers* in verse 28 [ἐπίσκοπος - episkopos] is the word from which we get the term *bishop*. It is a position of oversight. The word employed to express their *care for* the church [ποιμαίνω - poimaino] gives us the word *pastor,* or shepherd. In fact, this passage is one of two in the New Testament that clearly ascribes the titles of pastor, bishop and elder to the same individual in the church. (The other is 1 Peter 5:1-3.)

Though every minister is charged with fidelity to sound doctrine and all believers are admonished to rebuke error, it is particularly a responsibility of the pastor/elder/bishop, who is charged with the doctrinal faithfulness of the church.⁴ It is a necessary aspect of shepherding the flock to protect it from ravenous wolves.

It is not so with the chaplain. Chaplaincy is largely a ministry of encouragement and comfort. The chaplain ministers

---

4   We will deal elsewhere with the consideration of the oversight of chaplains by a local church as demonstrated by the early New Testament churches throughout the book of Acts.

mostly to the un-churched or those who, by virtue of their circumstances, are at least temporarily separated from their church body. Usually, the chaplain functions with limited authority as in military chaplaincy where it is mandated that the chaplain possesses rank without command, or in law enforcement chaplaincy where the chaplain must defer to the authority of the police officer.

A chaplain is not a missionary, because he is not charged with planting a local church. The ministry of planting churches, I am convinced, corresponds more closely with the evangelist of Ephesians 4:11 than does the contemporary concept of a revivalist. Perhaps because of the commendable emphasis on missions in evangelical churches throughout the twentieth century, it is popular today for Christian ministers of all sorts to identify themselves as missionaries. Missions has been the breath of evangelistic churches for all of our lifetimes and though, alas, the fervor is fading somewhat, there is yet a compelling prominence placed on the great commission by those who understand and submit to scripture. There is a certain adventure and romance to missionary service. Bible-believing Christians are touched by the need, and churches take pride in their missionary budgets, seeking to increase them annually. It is no surprise, then, that many worthwhile and much needed ministries insist upon identifying their workers as missionaries. The practice has become so commonplace that many of those who employ the term incorrectly, do so in all sincerity. There are "missionaries" to hospitals, sports teams, children, the down and out, motorcyclists, students, prisoners, the retarded, gambling casinos, and recreational areas to name a few. Non-profit "mission agencies" conduct sports clinics, sponsor evangelistic crusades, promote educational seminars and offer legal or financial services. These are often valuable and much needed ministries that honor God, but they are not missions. Missions is evangelization by means of the proclamation of the Gospel with the intent to establish a local church or churches in which the ordinances of the church are observed and converts are built up in the faith. In missions, the entire aspect of the great commission is in view, not just a specialized interest. "Go therefore and make disciples of all nations, baptizing them in the name of the Father and of the Son and of the Holy Spirit, teaching them to observe all that I have commanded you. And behold, I am with you always, to the end of the age."[5] Missions may appropriately include supplemental services for missionaries, such as administrative needs, assistance in missionary deputation, publications, and *et cetera* that support the church planting objectives. Chaplains are not typically engaged in establishing churches and are; therefore, not properly identified as missionaries.[6]

A chaplain ministers largely to those who live and work in a secular environment and, alas, sometimes have no church home or even knowledge of Christian truth. Christian chaplaincy, whether it be military, law enforcement, hospital, prison, athletic, corporate or whatever, functions as an important evangelistic and encouraging arm of the church, providing a reminder of the Providence of God and a conduit to the truth of God. Ideally, like the evangelist [missionary] he is charged with the announcement of the Gospel and like the pastor and the evangelist, he is held accountable to the church for doctrinal purity.[7]

Chaplain comes from an Old French word, *cappella,* which refers to the chapel. Originally it described one who had charge of a chapel, but the term has been understood in various ways over the centuries as the role of the chaplain has been modified to meet the needs of the times. There is no mention of the position in the Old Testament or New Testament, though we will see later that there are biblical examples of ministry descriptive of the modern day chaplain.

---

5   Matthew 28:19, 20

6   As is true of pastors, a missionary may also serve as a chaplain; however, they are two distinctly different though compatible ministries.

7   We will deal with this biblical requirement later as it will have particularly important bearing on the relationship of the chaplain to the local church.

A chaplain, in practical and current terms, is a clergyman who is appointed to bring the chapel to secular culture and institutions, ministering to those who are either un-churched, or separated from the immediate influence of a church. Interestingly, the title in its earliest uses was largely attributed to priests of the Roman Church, but in the present day most venues for chaplaincy bemoan the shortage of Catholic priests. Chaplaincy, today, is at least perceived to be somewhat dominated by ministers who espouse protestant[8] beliefs.[9] Chaplains, of necessity, minister in a pluralistic environment to people of all faiths or no faith. It is said to be a *Ministry of Presence*, because they bring a godly influence to the so-called secular arena – a reminder of the providence and provision of God.

The Encylopædia Britannica traces the history of chaplaincy from the 4th Century to the present:

> **"chaplain,** originally a priest or minister who had charge of a chapel, now an ordained member of the clergy who is assigned to a special ministry. The title dates to the early centuries of the Christian church.
>
> In the 4th century, chaplains (Latin *capellani*) were so called because they kept St. Martin's famous half cape (*capella*, diminutive of *cappa*). This sacred relic gave its name to the tent and later to the simple oratory or chapel where it was preserved. To it were added other relics that were guarded by chaplains appointed by the king during the Merovingian and Carolingian periods, and particularly during the reign of Charlemagne, who appointed clerical ministers (*capellani*) who lived within the royal palace. In addition to their primary duty of guarding the sacred relics, they

---

8 I am including in this overly broad category of Protestants, charismatic and Neo-Orthodox communions; Baptists and Free Churches who sometimes reject the label Protestant, but nevertheless identify with the broad intent of the reformers.

9 This may partially explain some of the opposition to chaplaincy on the part of some religious communions.

also said mass for the king on feast days, worked in conjunction with the royal notaries, and wrote any documents the king required of them. In their duties chaplains thus gradually became more identified with direct service to the monarch as advisers in both ecclesiastical and secular matters.

The practice of kings appointing their own chaplains spread throughout western Christendom. Many of the royal chaplains were appointed to bishoprics and the highest offices in the church; and down to the present day the British monarchs have appointed their own royal chaplains. British monarchs still appoint the members of the Royal College of Chaplains, whose duties now involve little more than preaching occasionally in the chapel royal.

In modern usage the term *chaplain* is not confined to any particular church or denomination. Clergy and ministers appointed to a variety of institutions and corporate bodies—such as cemeteries, prisons, hospitals, schools, colleges, universities, embassies, legations, and armed forces—usually are called chaplains.

Chaplains serve in the armed forces of most countries, generally as commissioned officers who are not required to bear arms. Protestant, Roman Catholic, and Jewish chaplains serve in the armed forces of the United States.

A chaplain performs basically the same functions in most armed forces. A chaplain in the U.S. military must furnish or arrange for religious services and ministrations, advise his commander and fellow staff officers on matters pertaining to religion and morality, administer a comprehensive program of religious education, serve as counselor and friend to the personnel of the command, and conduct instruction classes in the moral guidance program of his service."[10]

In the United States, chaplains are appointed at nearly every level of government from the Senate and House of Representatives to municipal police departments, as well as hospitals, prisons and jails. All branches of military service have highly developed and well respected chaplain programs. Most benevolent or fraternal organizations, service clubs and support groups have appointed chaplains; however, many of those so appointed may not be clergy and often have no formal ministerial training or experience.

Another practical way to define *chaplain* is to consider what a chaplain does. There are both similarities and differences in chaplaincy and what is commonly thought of as local church ministry. Generally speaking, the chaplain is appointed to help people cope with the unique circumstances of their profession or situation. Table 1 (next page) employs the acronym COPE to outline four common areas of chaplain ministry, the more specific duties that comprise them, and a comprehensive listing of expectations; however, some chaplaincies will not require or even allow all of these functions. The military chaplain, as an example, will probably be involved in nearly all of the elements noted, while a chaplain for a service club may only be tasked to offer prayer at an occasional luncheon. Hospital chaplaincy, usually based on a clinical pastoral education (CPE) model, is often more restrictive in its religious expression. Some chaplains are not authorized to perform or are uncomfortable with some of the ministerial expectations. For instance, a Protestant minister would be understandably uncomfortable offering last rites and would logically consider that function a referral under the heading of extending religious freedom instead of placing it in the category of pastoral ministry. A chaplain who was not trained

10 The New Encyclopædia Britannica, 15th ed., s.v. "chaplain."

Table 1

The COPE Acronym

Crisis Response	Official Functions	Pastoral Encouragement	Extend Religious Freedom
Crisis intervention	Advisor	Counseling	Referral to clergy
Physical Aid	Invocations	Worship Services	Religious
CISM	Benedictions	Hospital/Home visits	accommodation
Combat ministry and support	Civic ceremonies	Confidentiality	
	Special events	Trusted conversation	
Grief management	Appointments	Weddings	
Prayer	Promotions	Funeral/memorial services	
Referral	Retirements		
	Change of command	Baptism	
		Communion	
	Staff meetings	Last Rites	
	Prayer	Prayer	

in critical incident stress management (CISM) would be foolish to attempt a critical incident stress debriefing (CISD). Religious freedom extends to the recipient of chaplaincy to be sure, but also to the minister. That is why chaplains typically are not required to perform any duty that conflicts with their religious convictions. There are times when the chaplain will be compelled to say "No" or refer the matter to another.

Chaplains are most evident to the general population following trauma or a critical incident resulting in a crisis of some sort. Much of the culture will have no other contact with a minister. The chaplain's participation could be as simple as the provision of physical needs or as comprehensive as stress management or spiritual counseling. Chaplains are indelibly identified with crisis intervention and grief management. Though for many years the mental health community has been suspicious of ministers (and *vice versa*), there is an increasing awareness that crises of faith can be more effectively addressed by a spiritual or religious intervention, and it is not uncommon to find chaplains (ministers) and mental health professionals working together and/or cross referring.

Chaplains offer dignity and spiritual influence to official functions, civic and military ceremonies and special events. Invocations and benedictions are a reminder of the presence of God and His Providence. Chaplains often add distinctive recognition to appointments, promotion ceremonies and retirement celebrations. One of the most important functions of a chaplain in his official capacity is that of an advisor to the commander (in the military) or administrator (in the civic venue). The chaplain is often expected to provide wise counsel in matters of morality, morale and ethics and is often invited to sit in on staff meetings as a trusted consultant.

Pastoral encouragement is every effective chaplain's desire. Crisis response and official functions are the means to the end of rendering spiritual succor and guidance. Though the chaplain is not a pastor (as we have already noted) several pastoral opportunities are afforded the chaplain. These opportunities will vary dependent upon the type of chaplaincy and the expertise of the chaplain. In the military, chaplains provide ministry very similar to that of a church through a chapel program and field worship services. Prison chaplains may conduct worship services as well. Counseling is often required in any ministry. The assurance of confidentiality and/or trusted communication[11] is a valuable provision. Weddings and funerals or memorial services are much appreciated and offer the opportunity to broaden the chaplain's sphere of ministry. Hospital and home visitation provides solace and encouragement to the injured, sick and bereaved. Finally, chaplains sometimes

---

11 By the term "trusted communication" I mean to describe the situation in which the chaplain is privy to conversations that may not fit under the category of confidentiality, but, nevertheless, the expectation is that the discourse will be kept in confidence.

provide liturgical rites and church ordinances to those they serve. This is particularly true in prison and military venues and somewhat more infrequent in most other chaplaincies. Prayer is an important aspect of the activity of a chaplain and is applicable in every category of ministry.

Chaplains are often charged with the provision of religious freedom through religious accommodation. In military, law enforcement and hospital chaplaincy it is a mandated requirement. It is the proviso on which the continuation of chaplaincy rests in the face of persistent atheist challenges to any Christian witness in public life. Chaplains are able to minister to everyone by securing for all the religious freedoms and privileges guaranteed them by the Constitution and by long established tradition. Referral to clergy of disparate faith groups is expected of chaplains when the need arises. Military chaplains, in particular, are required to accommodate the religious needs of everyone placed under their care.

So then, by definition, a chaplain is a clergyman who is appointed to bring the chapel to secular culture and institutions, ministering to those who are either un-churched, or separated from the immediate influence of their church. In modern practice, a chaplain is a minister who is assigned to provide crisis response; encouragement; counsel and pastoral services; and the extension of religious freedom to those in the public or private arena who are grouped by a common assignment, culture or responsibility; usually associated through a military, government or benevolent agency.

That's a long detailed answer to the gentleman's question. The short version is this: A chaplain is a minister who represents the presence and interest of God in community and crisis.

In March of 2000, a new chaplain was appointed to the U.S. House of Representatives, continuing a tradition that began in 1774. Early in his tenure, as Chaplain Daniel P. Coughlin was walking through the House chambers, he was stopped by a stranger. "You're the new chaplain, aren't you," he said.

Chaplain Coughlin affirmed that he was. "You're a nobody," the man insisted. Before the chaplain could respond he went on to say: "That's right. You're a *no*body that is sent here to tell *every*body that there's a *some*body who can save *any*body." That's the best definition yet.

CHAPTER TWO

CHAPLAINCY DELINEATED

Among the challenges faced as a bible college student was a summer special project. God had provided me with part-time employment with the City as a swimming instructor, a position for which I had received much training for several years. All those seemingly wasted summer hours as a child splashing in Lake Washington and moving through the plethora of swimming classes had finally paid off. As a young Airman in military service, I had completed the Water Safety Instructor course and fulfilled my apprenticeship of teaching. Now, as a ministerial student, my employment enabled me to expand my experience through involvement with the Red Cross Water Safety program.

Then came the summer special project. A government grant to the City provided for portable swimming pools four feet deep to be placed in school yards of disadvantaged neighborhoods to offer swimming instruction to the young children who desired it. It was intended to provide a safe and beneficial summer outlet for a particular ethnic group in the community.[12] There was a problem; however, because the grant required the swimming instruction be provided by members of that ethnic group and there was not a single Water Safety Instructor in the entire County meeting that criteria. The chosen solution was to hire people who had little or no previous instruction or experience in water safety, and put them through a brief training to familiarize them with the various steps in

---

12   The identity of the ethnic group is of no importance and has little bearing on the point of the illustration.

the teaching process. I was chosen to provide that training and general oversight of the program.

I'm sure that many children were helped by the effort. Even the rudimentary elements of swimming are important factors in water safety and there can be no doubt that just learning how to float or tread water may someday save one's life. Imagine my dismay; however, when I visited one of the pools on a hot afternoon to find several small children unsupervised in a four foot deep swimming pool while the "instructor" (one of my students) was across the street purchasing an ice cream cone from a vendor, with his back to the pool. I immediately secured the pool and fired the instructor. There followed a political donnybrook that ended in his reinstatement and almost brought about my own dismissal for taking such precipitous action. As I looked back on the incident, it occurred to me that the problem was not that the instructor was incapable of teaching the rudimentary steps of swimming. I had seen to that. The real difficulty lay in the fact that he had been denied the years of water safety culture that would have drummed into his mindset that you never, never turn your back on a pool when you have the responsibility for the safety of its occupants. His brief training and desire to teach was commendable, but simply wasn't enough to provide him with the overall competence that only comes from the long-term process. He was a swimming teacher, of sorts, but not a Water Safety Instructor.

What does that story have to do with chaplaincy? It illustrates the way our culture sometimes views chaplaincy and the resulting unfortunate consequence of a careless evaluation of chaplain ministry. The question of who is qualified to be a chaplain is a perplexing one and sometimes difficult to address. In order to outline a biblical perspective, we must consider some contemporary elements of the issue that point to the need for a useful benchmark. The first of these is diversity.

Diversity is a good thing. It is found everywhere in God's creation. He has created each of us different in some fashion;[13] assigned to us variegated challenges[14] and differing gifts and responsibilities.[15] Diversity is often seen as a principal strength of chaplaincy, but it may also result in an adverse ambiguity if it lacks a consistent standard. The establishment of that standard is not an easy task to be sure, but a very necessary one. Multiplicity in chaplaincy is much more than a representation of people groups. There are a number of diversities to be considered.

The diversity of ministries is obvious. Chaplain programs will be found in the military services and their auxiliaries; police departments; fire services; hospitals and hospice care; service clubs; race tracks; gambling casinos; college and professional athletic teams; corporations and companies; beaches and resorts; the New Orleans French Quarter; cruise ships; prisons and jails; rescue missions and homeless projects; veterans organizations; colleges and universities; shopping centers; and Congress to cite only a partial list. Each has its own limited area of concern and those who minister may be familiar with the particular sphere of interest, yet possess a very limited theological acumen. A public safety chaplain, for instance, may be chosen because of his expertise as a firefighter, but have little or no ministerial training or experience. Surely, it makes sense to utilize the practical experience of qualified chaplains who have a unique understanding of the people to whom they minister. Experiencing, or having experienced, the day to day challenges that face those to whom they minister is a very real part of a ministry of presence. On the other hand, substituting common experience for competence in handling the Word of God presents a problem of significant concern. An understanding of the workplace does not necessarily equate to a competent spiritual ministry and *vice versa*. This mixture

---

13 Psalm 139:13-16
14 James 1:2,3
15 1 Corinthians 12:4-11

leaves us with a question of how to balance these important elements.

The diversity of faith groups and individuals engaged in chaplaincy is almost as staggering. Each possesses a somewhat unique vision, methodology and motive. Each sets their own objectives and standards sometimes reminiscent of the Old Testament book of Judges wherein it is said that "every man did that which was right in his own eyes," because "there was no king in Israel."[16] It is not hard to see that the diversity that characterizes the structure of most chaplaincies can itself be both a strength and a challenge to effective ministry. In a culture in which people can purchase ordination certificates from bogus online churches; internet spam offers college degrees in two weeks; some churches are willing to ordain their members upon request without adequate examination; and even some evangelical organizations purchase advertising to find people who want to be ordained; it has become increasingly more difficult to apply objective standards. It is hard to imagine an "ordination council" comprised of three or four ministers of incongruent theological systems, effectively examining a candidate for ministry to approve his doctrinal acuity, but such is sometimes the case.

A third aspect of chaplaincy pointing to a need for consistent criteria is *the diverse structure of chaplaincy programs.* Though Christian chaplaincy may occasionally be an outreach of a church or churches, the organizations served are seldom governed by church polity or scriptural teachings. A law enforcement chaplain, for instance, is usually responsible to a Chief of Police, Sheriff or other official who, typically, is not qualified or authorized to exercise any sort of spiritual oversight. In situations where an independent multi-denominational chaplaincy provides chaplain services for a secular agency or agencies, the diversity of church groups makes it difficult, at best, to oversee the life and ministry of its disparate members.

---

16 Judges 17:6 & 21:25 KJV

The military best manages this dilemma by establishing their own minimum qualifications and then requiring the chaplains to be responsible to their individual denominational chaplain commissions (endorsers) for spiritual oversight.

Finally, there is a *diversity of candidates* for chaplain service. There are three aspects of this consideration that underscore the wisdom of an objective standard for chaplaincy. The first of these is the reality that most chaplain ministries are voluntary in nature. Typically, wherever there is a real need, there is an accompanying necessity for recruiting more chaplains. Inasmuch as there are relatively few paid positions and fewer still full-time paid positions available, it becomes increasingly difficult to adequately staff a chaplaincy as it grows in size and effectiveness. The temptation, then, is to find less demanding ways to increase the pool of chaplains. It becomes more and more difficult to insist on wisely established criteria for qualification and the end result may be (and often is) a gradual declination to the lowest common denominator. Ultimately, the ministerial competency of the chaplaincy suffers, though the crisis response feature may continue to prosper.

The shortage of qualified volunteers is exacerbated by the demands of religious pluralism as it seeks an ever-increasing demonstration of alternative religious expression. Public agencies are acutely aware of an expectation of the separation of church and state and even Christian chaplaincies must be sensitive to these demands in our culture. It is rarely, if ever, possible to ascribe standards that are so narrow as to provide total doctrinal agreement or even a common methodology. Chaplaincies, often comprised of ministers of incongruent theological foundations, are little more competent to provide spiritual oversight of the life and ministry of its chaplains than the public agencies and institutions they serve. The sometimes unreasonable expectations of pluralism complicate the establishment of qualifications for ministerial service, further diluting the ministry pool and dictating an even more disparate chaplaincy. The ensuing concern that no one be offended by dogmatic religious expression may lead to the mutual acceptance of conflicting spiritual values as equal truths. The recipients of such ministry may be left with the impression that everyone is just on different, but equally valid, paths to God. This is a particularly disturbing outcome for Christian ministers who espouse the biblical teaching that salvation is only obtained through Jesus Christ. "And there is salvation in no one else, for there is no other name under heaven given among men by which we must be saved."[17]

One more consideration is the expanding pool of candidates who aspire to chaplaincy without adequate ministerial preparation. In a sense, this is a circular dilemma. The enticement to increase the number of chaplains by seeking a lower common denominator stimulates interest on the part of some who have not been called of God to ministry, but nonetheless desire the position, thus accelerating the declination of established criteria. The contemporary trend to water down the expectations for clergy and the realities of pluralistic demand have encouraged many who have not previously considered ministry, or who are not able or willing to submit to the requirements of their local church or denomination, to seek status as chaplain-clergy. A chaplain who lacks in-depth biblical training may be more likely to "minister" by means of popular religious slogans and unbiblical platitudes.

Let there be no misunderstanding in this regard. There are many dedicated, religious people who have good instincts; who are competent in crisis response; who simply have not been called to ministry and who may or may not possess the biblical expertise, temperament and experience required of clergy. They are wonderful folks who can and should be utilized in appropriate situations to bring comfort and encouragement to the bereaved and hurting in times of crisis. They can be trained to do so in a relatively brief time. In truth, an argument could be made that all

---

17 Acts 4:12

Christians are called to that kind of service. Like the swimming instructors hastily pressed into service in my summer project, they can respond to crisis; but short of a call to ministry, and the longer term education and ministry experience that produces the culture of ministry, they are not clergy, whether or not they are called "chaplain." It would be useful to coin another term for these marvelous, dedicated people. Perhaps *crisis response worker, crisis responder, caregiver*, or some other descriptive term would be preferable.

Why make such a distinction? We have no angst over the concept of a "lay preacher," who is gifted in expounding the scriptures. There is not, nor should there be, a concern over a layman (I prefer the term believer priest) who occupies the pulpit, so long as the Word of God is faithfully and accurately presented. There are many gifted Bible teachers and professors who are not ordained and I thank God for them. The First Century churches benefited from the ministry of Aquila and Priscilla who assisted Paul in Corinth and sailed with him to Ephesus[18] where they were able to teach the noted preacher Apollos "the way of God more accurately,"[19] and later opened their home for the establishment of a local church.[20] Aquila, a tentmaker, and his wife Priscilla, a godly woman, understood the scriptures, and any minister would be fortunate to have their fellowship and instruction. Why then is it important for a chaplain to have *bona fide* credentials? There are several expectations that, while not entirely unique to chaplaincy, are desirable to qualify an individual for effective chaplain ministry; and which underscore the advisability of meaningful ministerial qualifications. These expectations will suggest the qualities preferred of the candidate for chaplaincy.

The first and, perhaps, most obvious is the ***expectation of confidentiality***. Chaplains, by the very nature of their function,

18   Acts 18:2, 18

19   Acts 18:26

20   1 Cor 16:19

are privy to communication that is denied to others, often simply because of their presence when sensitive matters are discussed. Nothing will render a chaplaincy ineffective faster than a breech of confidentiality. Generally, there are two separate and distinct areas of confidentiality to be considered, one is practical and the other is legal

The first of these is confidential discourse, which we might term trusted or sensitive communication. There is a presumption that, unless otherwise stated, what is said to a chaplain will be held in confidence. It is not a legal matter, but a practical one. Most discussion that takes place does not qualify as clergy/penitent communication in a legal sense, but the expectation of confidentiality remains. Anyone may render this privilege, but it is the solemn duty of a chaplain. There is no legal protection in the courts, and its preservation is secured only by the degree of commitment on the part of the chaplain and his understanding with the communicant. The chaplain must determine the limits of confidence based on such factors as whether revelation of the information may prevent the commission of a crime or grave harm to the individual or another. Generally speaking, any discussion in the presence of a third party falls into this category. There is no legal protection in the courts.

The legal concept of confidentiality is called penitential communication, clergy/penitent privilege, or priest/penitent privilege. In most, if not all, states the clergyman is not required to reveal in court the conversation with a person who confesses to a crime or misdeed of some sort. In fact, when an accused claims clergy/penitent communication, the clergyman is prohibited from testifying. There are important qualifications; however, that must be understood. In some cases, even an ordained person may not be considered as clergy by the court. Confidentiality laws vary from state to state and include such considerations as the specific role in which the chaplain is functioning during the time that clergy/penitent communication takes place, and whether he is adhering to the expectations of his church or denomination. There are various criteria for what communication may (or must) be held in confidence that are established by the minister's ecclesiastical authority. For instance, a Roman Catholic priest is expected by his church to withhold from the court any confession of wrong doing without regard to the severity of the confession or the harm it may do to another individual. Others minister with the expectation that a violation of confidentiality may be justified if it prevents future, immanent and severe bodily injury or death. There are circumstances in which courts will find that the confidentiality laws do not apply, because the chaplain was not at the time functioning as a clergyman or that it was not the customary expectation of his church or denomination that he should do so. It has been said that there are as many different concepts of confidentiality as there are denominations, all of which may be taken into consideration when a court orders (or does not order) a chaplain to testify. Refusal to comply may result in the incarceration of the chaplain.

For these reasons, we do a disservice to an aspiring chaplain if we hastily ordain him for ministry and thrust him into the expectation of confidentiality without first ensuring the oversight and approval of a viable church body and *bona fide* clergical credentials. On the other hand, we do an equal injustice to the recipient of chaplain ministry if we are unable or unwilling to establish criteria for chaplaincy that can meet the many legal tests for confidentiality. Both the confessor and the advisor are put in legal jeopardy if we do so. Chaplaincies should take care to understand the specific State and Federal requirements in whatever jurisdiction they minister, and establish benchmarks for appointment that encompass both spiritual and legal considerations. Military chaplains fall under the Federal confidentiality laws and enjoy a greater degree of protection when conversing with or counseling military personnel.

Secondly, there is the *expectation of commission*. As with all clerical occupation, the chaplain is deemed to be an individual who has been called by God and successfully examined by a reputable church body. A beautiful example of this is found in Second Corinthians chapter 8, where Paul appeals to the church in Corinth to come to the assistance of the church in Jerusalem with the provision of physical needs, an action that is at least reminiscent of the ministry of chaplaincy. The persecution that had come upon the Judean churches had brought about many hardships and there was a need for charitable relief. The Macedonian churches had already shown their willingness to help and now Paul was sending Titus to assist the Corinthians in the demonstration of this important grace and to take their offering to Jerusalem. Assisting Titus in this ministry were two other brethren, one "appointed by the churches"[21] in Macedonia and another who had been "often tested and found earnest in many matters."[22] It is thought, with good reason, that one of them may have been Luke. Paul was anxious to assure the Corinthian believers that these men were truly committed to the work, hence his reference to the heart of Titus in verse 16 and his willingness to serve in verse 17. To further encourage the Corinthians, Paul bore witness that these men were "messengers of the churches."[23] There could be no doubt that these men were carefully chosen for their task and had evidenced their qualifications to perform it. A comparison of Acts 11:29, 30 with Galatians 2:1 leads us to believe that Titus, who headed the team, had previous experience with just such a task when he accompanied Paul and Barnabas to Jerusalem on a similar mission. Scripture, here, testifies that Titus was called, was obedient to the call and was competent for the job. If such credentials were deemed necessary by Paul for the simple matter of collecting and delivering an offering,

---

21   2 Corinthians 8:19
22   2 Corinthians 8:22
23   2 Corinthians 8:23

how much more might we exercise diligence in determining the fitness of one who is to engage in the proclamation of the Word of God and offer spiritual counsel during life's most critical moments? The assurance of these qualities was then and is now the examination and testimony of the churches that exercise ecclesiastical authority in the life and ministry of those who represent them.

Third is the *expectation of competence*. Chaplaincy deals with life where the rubber meets the road. A pastor typically ministers in the relative comfort of a local church in which there exists a similar understanding of spiritual truth. Often, he is able to consult with other pastors and may consider at length the difficulties that he is called upon to address. The chaplain, on the other hand, ministers in a climate wherein he seldom encounters a significant number of people who share his theological perspective and understanding. Chaplain ministry in crisis is most often conducted in an environment in which religious unanimity is somewhat unusual, and is commonly hostile. Early one morning a chaplain was called upon to respond to the death of a cancer patient who had been cared for by a Christian woman with whom she took room and board. The deceased woman was a Jehovah's Witness, but the caretaker was a Christian. Shortly after the chaplain arrived, two men from the Kingdom Hall entered the premise and called the Deputy Coroner aside. After a brief conversation, the Deputy related to the chaplain that they were insisting he be sent away. He agreed to leave the dead woman to the representatives of the Watchtower Society, but was able to effect an agreement allowing him to minister to the Christian caretaker. A wise solution to what might have resulted in unnecessary additional stress. Ministry under these conditions requires an expertise in both spiritual wisdom and biblical acumen.

Often there is no time for deliberation, consultation or study. The chaplain may never have another opportunity to minister to the individual or individuals confronted by the crisis. When one encounters a crisis of faith it may require a knowledge of comparative religion, Bible doctrine, spiritual counseling, systematic theology, practical theology, pastoral theology, ecclesiology, psychology, hamartiology, soteriology, or eschatology to name a few. A real life incident illustrates the need for all of these disciplines in response to a single, but complex question.

A young professional in a metropolitan city took his two children, ages three and five, to the hardware store late on a Saturday morning. His wife, also a professional, stayed home to rest. Returning about lunchtime, the young man prepared a meal for his children and then went upstairs to check on his wife. He found her in the bedroom where she had hung herself. Visibly shaken, he ran across the street to obtain assistance from his neighbor, who called the police. He returned home, and with the help of his neighbor, cut his wife down, laid her on the bed and waited for the police to arrive. A law enforcement chaplain was called and when he arrived he found the distraught husband seated on a bench in the dining room. His head was cradled in his hands in obvious distress. He did not look up or even acknowledge the chaplain's presence. The chaplain touched him lightly on the shoulder, identified himself, and sat quietly in an adjacent chair. After many seconds that seemed like several minutes, the distraught husband moaned. "Can she still go to heaven?"

That brief question called upon many areas of expertise. It was a theological question that demanded an understanding of soteriology. It suggested that, perhaps, the questioner had a Roman Catholic background and had been taught a different perspective than he might have learned in a Protestant, Baptist, Pentecostal or Free church [comparative religion & ecclesiology]. It obviously expressed a concern for the eternal state of the deceased [hamartiology]. It dealt with future things [eschatology]. It was an expression of grief and despair [psychology]. It was a plea for an illusive answer during a crisis of faith [pastoral theology]. It was a cry for solace in the face of unimaginable circumstances [spiritual counseling]. It called for a sensitive and meaningful response [practical theology]. To formulate a compassionate and truthful reply, the chaplain must draw upon knowledge in all these areas in addition to crisis intervention techniques. Even more challenging was the notification to small children of the death of their Mother, and answering their questions. Certainly, it is a situation that calls for competence in a wide range of theological and spiritual wisdom.

I do not mean to imply that it was the time for lengthy discourse on any of these important theological concerns, only that without an understanding of them, it would be difficult, if not unwise, to formulate a short, simple statement of assurance that takes into consideration the extensive spiritual and religious factors that contributed to the questioners dilemma. Experience would remind the chaplain that it is not the time for a sermon, but would also caution him that the wrong response might bring all of these concerns to a crescendo at a most inopportune moment when the questioner was in no condition to deal with them. Comprehensive theological training and practical ministry experience combine to meet the challenge.

Competence in chaplaincy demands a working knowledge of many denominations, faiths and backgrounds. The chaplain ministers to people of all religions and no religion. Seldom are there pat answers to the challenges and questions that are encountered, despite the plethora of platitudes that abound in the popular culture. What may encourage some may well be a discouragement to others who do not share the same understanding of God. Worse, a familiar proverb hastily offered may prove to be just the wrong spiritual advice at the time, leading the recipient into confusion. We often hear "God helps those who help themselves," as though it were taken from the pages of holy writ, but those who rely on that maxim as a guide in crisis will surely miss the succor that comes from complete dependence on God. A chaplain who lacks a solid grounding in the Word of God and biblical theology is likely to be drawn away from the truth by the socially attractive fiction of the world, and even unwittingly encourage a misleading gospel that denigrates the sovereignty of God. It is not uncommon, for instance, for a well-meaning comforter to make light of God as "the man upstairs," for fear of offending the hearer, with little consideration of the theological implications of presenting God so flippantly. Portraying the divine Providence of God as a "God thing," is a comparable trivialization of the Almighty. Such statements are, no doubt, offered in ignorance of such implications and without intending insult; however, all too often, little thought is given to the reputation of God. No one has yet been saved by "the man upstairs," but by the Sovereign Majesty whose justice was satisfied by nothing less than the incarnate God the Son offering Himself a deliberate sacrifice as decreed by God from before the foundation of the world.[24] The spiritual implication of flippant testimony underscores the desirability of a sound biblical and theological competence as a prerequisite for chaplain ministry.

Fourth, a chaplain must meet the *expectation of collaboration*. Chaplains minister largely in the secular world to and among those of many faiths or of no faith. It is a world fraught with danger for the immature that lack a thorough understanding of their beliefs. The demands placed upon them will often require religious understanding well beyond the boundaries of their church's expectations or polity. Routinely, they are required to work collegially with clergy who hold theological viewpoints with which they have disagreement. There are pitfalls awaiting the novice in that kind of situation. It calls for wisdom gleaned from a well-rounded biblical expertise, and maturity reinforced by wide-ranging ministry experience. In the absence of a comprehensive theological foundation there is a greater probability of misunderstanding or mishandling

---

24 Leviticus 19:12, 1 Peter 1:18-20, Acts 2:23

the circumstance or opportunity. Mistakes in crisis response are common and usually easily remedied, but when spiritual counseling and acumen are called for, the stakes are considerably higher. When dealing with the matter of eternal salvation, or a broken marriage, or solicitation to sin, an extensive biblical understanding is often essential.

A second concern is that a novice who lacks a well-rounded spiritual and biblical understanding may become susceptible to doctrinal error when exposed in an environment where differences are rarely challenged. Paul was careful to instruct the church in Ephesus in this regard. In Ephesians 4:11, he speaks of those that God had given to the church to provide for maturity and edification. The reason cited in verse 14 was so that they would "no longer be children, tossed to and fro by the waves and carried about by every wind of doctrine, by human cunning, by craftiness in deceitful schemes." The church was divinely equipped to provide for their spiritual growth and protect them from the many deceptions of false teachers. It is essential that a chaplain, who ministers largely in an arena that does not enjoy the immediate guardianship and encouraging reinforcement of a church, be adequately prepared.

There is probably no area of ministry that exceeds chaplaincy in the *expectation of consolation*. It is not uncommon for people to associate chaplaincy almost exclusively with tragic circumstances such as death notifications, traumatic occurrences and mass casualties. It is assumed that the chaplain will bring comfort and solace to the recipients of bad news. This somewhat obvious truth is aptly illustrated by Chaplain Tom Webb, a U.S. Navy Reserve chaplain and chaplaincy consultant in San Diego, who writes of the unique value of the chaplain's ministry of presence:

> "Often a pastoral crisis interventionist affects a significant mitigation of traumatic stress by simply being recognized and being present. For

example, a person who had just experienced the unexpected loss of a loved one experiences a sense of hope and relief as they recognize the presence of the chaplain or pastor and exclaim, 'The chaplain is here!' The weight of the world in that moment of exclamation seems to lessen from the person in despair. The person *out of the dark pit of destruction in which they feel mired* can sense some hope that they will be able to function again as a whole person through their being connected with their spiritual resources. Through the horizontal connection with the pastoral crisis interventionist an individual gains hope to be able to renew trust and dialog in relationships with family, friends, and co-workers."[25]

One might ask what prepares a person for such a healing presence. Surely, there are qualities to be cultivated in preparation for ministry through sustained dependence upon God in difficult challenges.

The classic New Testament passage concerning a ministry of comfort is found in 2 Corinthians 1:3, 4, "Blessed be the God and Father of our Lord Jesus Christ, the Father of mercies and God of all comfort, who comforts us in all our affliction, so that we may be able to comfort those who are in any affliction, with the comfort with which we ourselves are comforted by God." It is interesting to note that the consolation of which Paul wrote was somewhat broad. He spoke of the comfort we receive from Christ in "<u>all</u> our affliction" and then offered assurance that it was sufficient to minister to "those who are in <u>any</u> affliction," as well as those who endure the <u>same</u> afflictions as did Paul and his companions. It is not always necessary to have experienced the same tribulation or trouble to avail oneself of the same comfort

25   International Journal of Emergency Mental Health, Vol. 3, Number 3, Summer, 2001

of God, but there certainly is an implication that the one who is called upon to comfort is likely to endure affliction of some sort in preparation for such a ministry. Though it does not explain every reason for the difficult circumstances in our lives, it does provide us with an understanding of one compelling reason that helps us to embrace trials with a view toward glorifying God through ministry to others. This passage points to "the God of all comfort," in reiterating, "we ourselves are comforted by God." There is little doubt that the presence of a representative of God is an effective agent for solace in tragedy. But that man of God must himself possess a degree of spiritual maturity that will enable him to face difficult, even heartbreaking circumstances and remain faithful in his walk with God.

Such a man was Job who faced almost unimaginable personal trauma and gave us one of the most compelling models of faithfulness in history. In that regard, Job's example epitomized what it means to minister in crisis. He would have made a fine chaplain. It is a familiar account. Job was a man of substance with a loving family. Life was good. At least it was until in rapid succession his wealth was stolen, his children were killed and his health failed. We find Job grieving in the dirt, covered with boils, enduring the criticism of a distressed wife. In all that, scripture tells us, Job did not sin[26] and he remained faithful. That man can certainly bring consolation in a meaningful way.

We cannot say that such tragedy is necessarily a prerequisite to ministry, but often it is. A man's mettle is tested in such circumstances, proving the validity of his faith. The Lord Jesus reminded those who would follow Him that they would have to forfeit the comfort of hearth and home.[27] He further warned them, "No man, having put his hand to the plough, and looking back, is fit for the kingdom of God." Peter learned that principle and later wrote to the Christians who were scattered by persecution:

---

26 Job 1:20-22
27 Luke 9:57-62

"do not be surprised at the fiery trial when it comes upon you to test you, as though something strange were happening to you. But rejoice insofar as you share Christ's sufferings..."[28] Timothy was admonished to understand that the proof of his ministry was at least partially validated by his consistency when called upon to "endure suffering."[29] We do no favor to one who aspires to ministry if we thrust him into the battle with inadequate spiritual preparation. It might further be said that doing so places the novice in some measure of jeopardy.

The account of Job's tribulations is impressive, but of equal note is the examination of those characteristics that prepared him to endure such contradiction and remain faithful. The first five verses of Job give us five descriptors that are helpful in understanding how he was able to trust in God so completely under such difficult circumstances.

> There was a man in the land of Uz whose name was Job, and that man was blameless and upright, one who feared God and turned away from evil. [2] There were born to him seven sons and three daughters. [3] He possessed 7,000 sheep, 3,000 camels, 500 yoke of oxen, and 500 female donkeys, and very many servants, so that this man was the greatest of all the people of the east. [4] His sons used to go and hold a feast in the house of each one on his day, and they would send and invite their three sisters to eat and drink with them. [5] And when the days of the feast had run their course, Job would send and consecrate them, and he would rise early in the morning and offer burnt offerings according to the number of them all. For Job said, "It may be that my children have sinned, and cursed God in their hearts." Thus Job did continually. Job 1:1-5

---

28   1 Peter 4:12,13
29   2 Timothy 4:5

Job, we are told, was "blameless." In the modern vernacular we would say that he was a man of integrity. It would be difficult to bring a charge against him. He was "upright," meaning he was a straight shooter. He "feared God." There was a deep reverence borne of an awareness of the sovereignty of God. He "turned away from evil." That means he put away evil from his life. Job practiced his faith before his family where it was most visible. He regularly made offerings for his children; prayed for them and showed genuine concern for their relationship with God. He was consistent in his testimony. Such was the man who God would use to demonstrate His grace. Integrity, honesty, reverence toward God, avoidance of evil and consistent religious affection are graces that ought to characterize the servant of God. They are not developed instantly, but result from the consistently demonstrable growth of a "new creation"[30] in Christ. It should not be lost to the reader that Job had demonstrated these virtues over a long period of time. He had ten adult children.

Paul spoke of believers who were not yet ready for the meatier nourishment expected of the mature Christian, for they were still behaving in a worldly way.[31] He further cautioned us against thrusting a "recent convert" into ministry, lest he "become puffed up with conceit and fall into the condemnation of the devil."[32] We do a disservice to the novice who desires to obtain ministerial validation through becoming a chaplain when we place him in this spiritual danger.

A similar and vital requisite for chaplaincy is the ***expectation of character.*** Paul instructed Timothy that there are sorrows that we can bring upon ourselves. In his first letter to Timothy, he referenced those who had "pierced themselves through with many sorrows"[33] as a result of their focus on the accumulation of wealth. Rather, he wrote, the "man of God" was

---

30 2 Corinthians 5:17
31 1 Corinthians 3:1-3
32 1 Timothy 3:6
33 1Timothy 6:10 KJV

to "pursue righteousness, godliness, faith, love, steadfastness, gentleness."[34] The Apostle James adds an admonition concerning lust, insisting "each person is tempted when he is lured and enticed by his own desire."[35] The Apostle John summarizes these and ties them together saying, "all that is in the world – the desires of the flesh and the desires of the eyes and pride in possessions – is not from the Father, but is from the world."[36] That's what the world offers and it is always detrimental to the testimony of the man of God. That is; however, the very arena in which the chaplain usually ministers. He brings a testimony of God into the secular culture, where Christian integrity and character are challenged daily. It is vital that he be solidly grounded in the Word of God and experienced in the walk of faith. It is the scripture that provides "teaching,… reproof,… correction, and… training in righteousness, that the man of God may be competent, equipped for every good work."[37] Therefore, it is absolutely essential that candidates for Christian chaplaincy have a comprehensive biblical understanding.

It is tragic to read almost daily of a chaplain that has fallen into sin. It is not a problem unique to chaplaincy by any means; however, one wonders if such poor representation of Christianity might have been avoided by a more diligent consideration of chaplain qualifications at the outset. A Google search for articles concerning chaplaincy will almost daily bring news such as charges being brought against a Kentucky jail chaplain after pornography was found on his computer; an Ohio police chaplain who pleaded guilty to fifty-four counts of having sex with girls under fifteen; a Michigan chaplain arrested for assault with a deadly weapon in a road rage incident; or a California chaplain, depressed over marital problems, who confessed to driving under the influence of alcohol. Aberrations to be sure, certainly outweighed by the preponderance of good

---

34 1 Timothy 6:11
35 James 1:14,15
36 1 John 2:16
37 2 Timothy 3:16, 17

that is accomplished by chaplains, but such extreme cases might have been avoided by a more careful examination of the applicants suitability for ministry. When individuals with questionable character are admitted into ministry, the testimony of God is sullied and above all, we ought to be zealous for the Name of God and His glory.

This is not to say that one who at any time in the past was struck down by sin is forever disqualified for chaplaincy. Second Timothy 2:20, 21 offers instruction and hope for such a person. "Now in a great house there are not only vessels of gold and silver but also of wood and clay, some for honorable use, some for dishonorable. Therefore if anyone cleanses himself from what is dishonorable, he will be a vessel for honorable use, set apart as holy useful to the master of the house, ready for *every good work*." (Emphasis mine) The contrast here is not that of gold, silver, wood and clay, but of honorable vessels and dishonorable vessels. How vastly superior it is to be a wood or clay vessel in honorable use than a gold or silver one in dishonorable pursuit. The cleansed and repentant testimony of a child of God who has once fallen from honor and endured the chastening of the Lord resulting in true repentance and a proven life can be just the encouragement needed by others. To be sure, such a vessel must be tested for an extended time, examined by the church and found to be competent in truth, testimony and theology.

No doubt, some may object to ever again entrusting such a person with spiritual ministry. There are good and godly theologians on both sides of the issue and we will not settle it in this book. But I cannot overlook the conclusion of Second Timothy 2:21 in its declaration that the believer who is thus cleansed from that which was dishonorable, is set apart by God, and is proven to be an honorable vessel is thereby "ready for every good work" [παν εργον αγαθον]. Nor can I find a limitation in view of the identical statement in Second Timothy 3:16, 17 indicating that Scripture equips the man of God "for every good work." Not to mention other identical uses of the term in First Timothy 5:10, Colossians 1:10, Titus 1:16, 3:1 and Hebrews 13:21. This assertion; however, does not absolve the minister of other considerations for adequate preparation, and most certainly requires a suitable and lasting demonstration of virtuous qualities outlined in scripture.

In view of the importance of the foregoing expectations, it is clear that there must also be some objective measure of qualification that encompasses the biblical admonition for godliness and the practical challenges of ministry. The military attempts this through requiring a Master of Divinity degree, valid ordination, pastoral experience and the formal endorsement of a denominational agency listed by the Department of Defense and charged with the spiritual oversight of the chaplain. These have proven to be the most stringent and the most effective criteria in common use, albeit based on a somewhat outdated model that was initially adopted before the advent of Bible institutes and colleges.

The requirement of a Master of Divinity degree verifies that the applicant for chaplaincy has *bona fide* religious educational training, but it makes no provision for matriculation at a bible institute or bible college. The assumption is made that the only path to ministerial education is by means of a bachelor degree in general education necessitating further study at a seminary to obtain the biblical and theological expertise for ministry. It is not unreasonable to consider a baccalaureate degree from a Bible college as equivalent to the content of a seminary degree if it includes the same theological courses. Many Bible colleges even include study in the original languages in their offerings. Some extend a baccalaureate degree an additional year for theological studies. There is some wisdom in requiring a Master's degree; however, if only to provide more time for the student to mature.

Another concern that complicates the evaluation of prospective chaplains is the requirement for ordination. It is a wise and very necessary prerequisite; however, there are a plethora of standards for ordination. Though there is general agreement in the educational community as to what constitutes an accredited college or seminary degree, there is no such consistency with regard to what standards one must meet to obtain ministerial licensing or ordination. It is possible to go online and purchase an ordination certificate for about thirty-five dollars[38] that will be recognized by the government. Some church bodies are willing to ordain their members for chaplaincy upon mere request, and some others do so without a meaningful ministerial education or examination. As noted previously, there are some interdenominational and nondenominational organizations that advertise for people to seek ordination and/or certification as a chaplain – for a fee. In some instances, there is a form of examination conducted by chaplains of disparate faiths or denominations, making it difficult if not impossible to scrutinize many important doctrinal views of the candidate. It is doubtful that an ordination certificate, without some evaluation of its source, will provide chaplaincies with adequate assurance of competence.

It has been said that experience is the best teacher. There is some validity to that platitude if we make the assumption that the experience is adequate, but there is a vast difference between someone who has five years of experience and someone who has one year of experience repeated five times. (My wife, a music teacher, once corrected me when I remarked "practice makes perfect." "No," she insisted, "perfect practice makes perfect.") In this day when nearly everything performed by a Christian is termed a "ministry," experience (practice) can be misleading. There are "ministries" to care for the pets of vacationers; "ministries" to surfers on the beach; "ministries" to provide financial services to the poor; "ministries" to send books to ministers; "ministries" to provide business management to

---

38   It is also possible to purchase a college degree online; however, I doubt if those degrees would be found acceptable in very many venues. On the other hand, there is a reluctance to reject the validity of a religious certification for fear of the accusation of discrimination.

churches; and so forth. I do not question the motive, compassion or value of those who engage in such activity, but one must ask if this kind of experience qualifies or enhances ones ability as a chaplain. Though worthwhile in some degree, they may not require any real biblical or theological expertise. Often, there is no oversight by a responsible church or denomination; no examination of the participants; no accountability for their "ministry;" and no doctrinal requirement for participation. Admittedly, it is difficult for secular institutions that employ chaplains to make judgments about the quality of religious endeavor, which in turn makes it problematical to place a value on experience when considering someone for chaplaincy. It is, therefore, wise to require pastoral experience in a venue that can be evaluated for legitimacy and effectiveness.

It bears repeating yet again that chaplaincy generally functions in a secular environment and utilizes ministers of diverse denominations and/or faith groups. For that reason, it is somewhat uncommon for additional theological training to be provided by chaplaincies. Doctrinal and spiritual oversight is dependent upon the oversight of the church or denomination. In that regard, the military model of requiring the chaplain to be responsible to an endorsing agency is commendable, though I would prefer accountability to a local church rather than a denominational agency.[39] Alas, few chaplaincies hold their workers to a specific doctrinal standard. Their statements of belief are usually deliberately brief and overly broad in scope to accommodate the disparity of its membership. In common practice, the agency (whether police or fire department; hospital; jail or prison; service club, veterans organization or whoever) provides guidance in crisis response and agency procedures, but is not commonly in a position to oversee the spiritual life and ministry of the chaplain. For that reason, it is essential that there be some assurance of a properly constituted religious authority to fulfill that important function.

---

39 More on this in a subsequent chapter

Military chaplaincy has a long established and effective criterion for selecting chaplains. Hospitals typically require certification in clinical pastoral education (CPE) for their paid chaplains, but are often more ambiguous about the standards for volunteer chaplains. Law enforcement, public service, corporate, and similar chaplaincies often lack a clear and objective means of evaluating ministry qualifications for chaplains. There is a need for established spiritual/theological criteria to measure the suitability of a chaplain applicant. These criteria should include a real theological education, *bona fide* credentials, proven ministerial experience and provision for spiritual oversight. With that in mind, may I humbly suggest the following:

1. At least three years of formal theological training in a reputable bible institute, bible college or seminary
2. Formal ordination by a properly constituted and recognized local church or denomination
3. Five years of *bona fide* pastoral experience
4. Formal endorsement and continuing oversight by the candidates local church or denominational chaplain endorsing agency

To the above spiritual considerations, each agency should add the additional requirements needed to qualify for the specific duties expected of them.

Concerning these suggestions, some may ask why someone who has been appointed as chaplain for a service club whose duties consist of saying a prayer at the periodic luncheon needs to have such stringent credentials. In fact, they don't, but in those instances they are not functioning as a minister involved in exposition of scripture, counseling, or the performance of sacerdotal duties. What is needed is a different term for that kind of ministry. Some have suggested *religious coordinator* or *prayer chairman*. None of those seem to fill the bill in every such instance. More thought should be given to this designation.

CHAPTER THREE

"WHO WILL GO FOR US?"

"For consider your calling, brothers: not many of you
were wise according to worldly standards, not many
were powerful, not many were of noble birth."
1 Corinthians 1:26

There is an old story about a young farmer who desired
to enter the ministry. One day he took a respite from plowing
his cornfield to enjoy the breeze in a shady spot beside the
field. As he lay on the ground looking up into the sky, he began
to study the cloud formations. Suddenly, he thought, a cloud
broke apart into three pieces and formed the letters G P C in
the sky. "Eureka," he thought, "this is a message from God. It's
the answer I've been looking for. GPC surely means go preach
Christ." He abandoned his farming, went off to Bible College
and entered the pastorate, but his ministry was fraught with
misfortune and failure. After many years of discouragement and
depression he confessed his unhappiness to an older preacher.
He related the story of his "call" to ministry some years before as
he was resting beside the cornfield. "Have you ever considered,"
the wise mentor said, "that the GPC you saw in the sky while
you were resting from your work in the field might rather have
meant go plow corn?"

There is a call to ministry. It is true that all believers
are charged with the proclamation of the Gospel and the
responsibility to glorify God in all that they do, but there can
be little doubt that there is also a specific call to the avocation
of ministry. The Lord Jesus called the twelve and trained them

as Apostles. The Holy Spirit set apart Barnabas and Saul for the work of ministry.[40] Ephesians 4:11 clearly teaches the Lord Jesus gave evangelists and pastor-teachers as a gift to the church. Timothy and Titus were given direction concerning the spiritual requirements of the office. Those who served faithfully were counted worthy of double honor.[41] Hebrews 13:17 insists that those who are called to oversee the church were to give an account for those who were entrusted to them. Admittedly, most of these references are specifically applied to the role of the pastor-teacher. A question might be raised as to whether a Christian chaplain is to be considered divinely called clergy or viewed as sub-clergy with less demanding expectations such as a specific call of God to ministry. The common requirement that chaplains be ordained would point to the former. Typically, the first two questions asked of a candidate for ordination seek a testimony of the applicant's salvation and an accounting of his call to ministry. The all too common practice in some agencies of appointing as chaplains men and women with little or no ministerial training or experience would suggest the latter. Surely, the answer to these questions lies in scripture, rather than the sometimes flawed practice of chaplaincies or institutions.

It is a fair question to ask whether we should employ the term "vocational ministry," (often expressed as "full-time Christian service") to the position of chaplain. Some would insist upon the term "professional," however this author would carefully avoid the term. John Piper ably and correctly insists:

> "The mentality of the professional is not the mentality of the prophet. It is not the mentality of the slave of Christ. Professionalism has nothing to do with the essence and heart of the Christian ministry. The more professional we long to be, the more spiritual death we will leave in our wake.

---

40 Acts 13:2
41 1 Tm 5:17

For there is no professional childlikeness (Matt. 18:3); there is no professional tenderheartness (Eph 4:32); there is no professional panting after God (Ps 42:1)."

But our first business is to pant after God in prayer. Our business is to weep over our sins (James 4:9). Is there professional weeping? Our business is to strain forward to the holiness of Christ and the prize of the upward call of God (Phil 3:14); to pummel our bodies and subdue them lest we be cast away (1 Cor 9:27); to deny ourselves and take up the blood-spattered cross daily (Lk 9:23). How do you carry a cross professionally? We have been crucified with Christ; yet now we live by faith in the one who loved us and gave Himself for us (Gal 2:20). What is professional faith?

We are to be filled not with wine but with the Spirit (Eph 5:18). We are God-besotted lovers of Christ. How can you be drunk with Jesus professionally? Then, wonder of wonders, we were given the gospel treasure to carry in clay pots to show that the transcendent power belongs to God (2 Cor 4:7). Is there a way to be a professional clay pot?"[42]

How then should we describe ministry and the call to it? Perhaps the best efforts have resulted in the term *vocational ministry,* but some would equate that only with full-time paid positions, leaving little room for "tentmakers" who, like the Apostle Paul, find it necessary or desirable to supplement their income with other pursuits; yet are nonetheless called of God to become what is commonly referred to as clergy. There is no comprehensive term in common use that has supplanted vocational ministry, though I would suggest a better description

---

42 John Piper, *Brothers, We are Not Professionals, A Plea to Pastors for Radical Ministry,* (Nashville: Broadman and Holman Publishers, 2002), 1-2

might be found in the idiom *divinely appointed ministry*. By that, I mean ministry originating in a divine call from God (the leading of the Holy Spirit); acknowledgement by the one so called (submission to the call); and the recognition of the church (commissioning). This chapter will examine the biblical replica of the modern day chaplain and consider its association with the call to divinely appointed ministry.

The word "chaplain" is not found in scripture, nor is there a clearly defined office which corresponds to chaplaincy. What we do find in the Bible are accounts of people who do what chaplains do. There are numerous examples. In Exodus chapter 17, for instance, we find Aaron and Hur performing a task reminiscent of the military chaplain.

> [9] So Moses said to Joshua, "Choose for us men, and go out and fight with Amalek. Tomorrow I will stand on the top of the hill with the staff of God in my hand." [10] So Joshua did as Moses told him, and fought with Amalek, while Moses, Aaron, and Hur went up to the top of the hill. [11] Whenever Moses held up his hand, Israel prevailed, and whenever he lowered his hand, Amalek prevailed. [12] But Moses' hands grew weary, so they took a stone and put it under him, and he sat on it, while Aaron and Hur held up his hands, one on one side, and the other on the other side. So his hands were steady until the going down of the sun. [13] And Joshua overwhelmed Amalek and his people with the sword." Exodus 17:9-13

As Israel faced their first real battle with Amalek, General Moses stood on the hill raising the rod of God, but his arms grew weary. Aaron and Hur ministered to him in a tangible way and the battle was won. Military chaplains would find that story familiar as they remember their ministry of encouragement to soldiers in combat.

Exodus chapter 18 recounts the ministry of Jethro, a priest of Midian and Father-in-Law to Moses who ministered in a fashion similar to the chaplain's role as advisor to the authorities.

8 Then Moses told his father-in-law all that the LORD had done to Pharaoh and to the Egyptians for Israel's sake, all the hardship that had come upon them in the way, and how the LORD had delivered them. 9 And Jethro rejoiced for all the good that the LORD had done to Israel, in that he had delivered them out of the hand of the Egyptians.

10 Jethro said, "Blessed be the LORD, who has delivered you out of the hand of the Egyptians and out of the hand of Pharaoh and has delivered the people from under the hand of the Egyptians. 11 Now I know that the LORD is greater than all gods, because in this affair they dealt arrogantly with the people." 12 And Jethro, Moses' father-in-law, brought a burnt offering and sacrifices to God; and Aaron came with all the elders of Israel to eat bread with Moses' father-in-law before God.

13 The next day Moses sat to judge the people, and the people stood around Moses from morning till evening. 14 When Moses' father-in-law saw all that he was doing for the people, he said, "What is this that you are doing for the people? Why do you sit alone, and all the people stand around you from morning till evening?" 15 And Moses said to his father-in-law, "Because the people come to me to inquire of God; 16 when they have a dispute, they come to me and I decide between one person and another, and I make them know the statutes of God and his laws." 17 Moses' father-in-law said to him, "What you are doing is not good. 18 You and the people with you

will certainly wear yourselves out, for the thing is too heavy for you. You are not able to do it alone. [19] Now obey my voice; I will give you advice, and God be with you! You shall represent the people before God and bring their cases to God, [20] and you shall warn them about the statutes and the laws, and make them know the way in which they must walk and what they must do. [21] Moreover, look for able men from all the people, men who fear God, who are trustworthy and hate a bribe, and place such men over the people as chiefs of thousands, of hundreds, of fifties, and of tens. [22] And let them judge the people at all times. Every great matter they shall bring to you, but any small matter they shall decide themselves. So it will be easier for you, and they will bear the burden with you. [23] If you do this, God will direct you, you will be able to endure, and all this people also will go to their place in peace."

[24] So Moses listened to the voice of his father-in-law and did all that he had said. [25] Moses chose able men out of all Israel and made them heads over the people, chiefs of thousands, of hundreds, of fifties, and of tens. [26] And they judged the people at all times. Any hard case they brought to Moses, but any small matter they decided themselves. Exodus 18:8-26

Chaplains often perform duties similar to that of Jethro as they come along side the secular authorities to encourage and advise them in matters of faith and morality. It's significant to note that Jethro brought sacrifices for God and his wisdom was applied to matters of government. He reinforced the perception that it was God that had delivered them and he even offered a mild rebuke in counseling Moses to make a priority of attending to the things of God.

In Deuteronomy chapter 20, Moses is outlining to the people of Israel the conventions of warfare. Israel would yet face many battles and the army was of utmost importance. In Numbers 1:17-46 a draft had been established consisting of every male from the age of 20 who was able to go to war. Israel raised an army of 603,550 soldiers. Now they were to learn the rules for engaging in warfare as God had revealed them to Moses, and the first rule was the appointment of a priest who functioned like a chaplain.

"When you go out to war against your enemies, and see horses and chariots and an army larger than your own, you shall not be afraid of them, for the LORD your God is with you, who brought you up out of the land of Egypt. ² And when you draw near to the battle, *the priest shall come forward and speak to the people* ³ *and shall say to them*, 'Hear, O Israel, today you are drawing near for battle against your enemies: *let not your heart faint. Do not fear or panic or be in dread of them, ⁴ for the LORD your God is he who goes with you to fight for you against your enemies, to give you the victory.*'" Deuteronomy 20:1-4 (Emphasis mine)

From these early times, it has been the practice of God's people to seek spiritual encouragement in the face of anticipated battle. In Numbers 31:6, we are told "And Moses sent them to the war, a thousand from each tribe, together with Phinehas the son of Eleazar the priest, with the vessels of the sanctuary and the trumpets for the alarm in his hand." In the United States of America, we have followed a similar model from the very beginning of our nation, with chaplains appointed to the Continental Army, and we continue to do so to the present day. No war has ever been fought by the United States without the presence of chaplains to encourage and minister to the troops.

The function, if not the title, of chaplaincy is made abundantly clear in the New Testament. In order to encourage the Christians in Colossae, the Apostle Paul sent "a faithful minister and fellow servant in the Lord" named Tychicus. Colossians 4:7-8 explains his mission: "Tychicus will tell you all about my activities. He is a beloved brother and faithful minister and fellow servant in the Lord. **8 I have sent him to you for this very purpose**, that you may know how we are and **that he may encourage your hearts**…" (emphasis mine) What makes this statement remarkable and applicable to chaplaincy is the purpose of Tychicus' visit. He was to comfort them. The word *encourage* here is from παρακαλεω [parakaleo]. It means *to call to one's side*. Tychicus was one who was called alongside to help the Colossians by bringing them encouragement. What better description can one have of the work of chaplaincy? The same basic word is employed two times by the Lord Jesus in John chapter 14. During the precious time of fellowship with His disciples just before the events of Gethsemane and Golgotha, Jesus sought to comfort them. He spoke of his departure and all were aware of the danger, but He assured them that He would not leave them orphans. He promised to send another Comforter [παρακλητον – parakleton] in verse 16, and again in verse 26 He identified that Comforter as the Holy Spirit, the Divine One called alongside to help. That's what chaplains do. In the tradition and power of the Holy Spirit, they bring recognition of the presence of God to encourage in times of crisis and blessing.

The use of the word in Colossians 4:8 implies to us that Tychicus was *called* to his ministry – he was *called* alongside to help. Verse 7 has already identified him as a beloved brother, a minister [διακονασ – diakonos], and a fellow servant [συνδουλοσ – syndoulos] with Paul. Diakonos is used in the New Testament to refer to a deacon,[43] to a government official[44] and as one who serves a high official.[45] Though the word is used

43   1 Timothy 3:8
44   Romans 16:1
45   Matthew 22:13

of the office of deacon, it is by no means limited to that position. Easton's Bible Dictionary says of this word: "Greek diaconos, usually a subordinate officer or assistant employed in relation to the ministry of the gospel, as to Paul and Apollos (1 Cor 3:5), Tychicus (Eph 6:21), Epaphras (Col 1:7), Timothy (1 Thes 3:2), and also to Christ (Rom 15:8)." [46] This citing presents Tychicus in a ministry role with Paul, on a par with Apollos, Epaphras and Timothy. Apollos was a gifted preacher who followed Paul in the pulpit in Corinth. Epaphras was a prominent figure as well. J.B. Lightfoot says of him: "We gather that Epaphras evangelized the cities of the Lycus valley in Phrygia under Paul's direction during the latter's Ephesian ministry, and founded the churches of Colossae, Hierapolis and Laodicea."[47]   Timothy, was a protégé of the Apostle Paul and became the pastor of the church in Ephesus. All three of these men, like Tychicus, were said to be fellow laborers or fellow servants with Paul." Fellow servant [sundoulos], in this context, implies someone who is mutually engaged in the same servanthood.   In plain English, Tychicus was one who was called out and engaged in the same service as Paul. That in itself is a strong indication of a divinely appointed ministry. Tychicus was sent on a mission to the church in Ephesus.[48] It would appear that he was not a pastor-teacher, but was given several important missions for the purpose of encouraging the brethren. As a fellow minister with the Apostle, his presence lent a measure of credibility to the endeavor.

It is believed that Paul sent Tychicus to return the escaped slave Onesimus, named in Colossians 4:9, to his master Philemon. Certainly, Onesimus accompanied him to Colossae and is also called a "beloved brother;" however, it is not said of him that he is a fellow minister with Paul, giving weight to

---

46   Easton, M. (1996, c1897). *Easton's Bible dictionary*. Oak Harbor, WA: Logos Research Systems, Inc.

47   J. B. Lightfoot, *St Paul's Epistles to the Colossians and to Philemon*, 1879, pp. 29ff.

48   Ephesians 6:21,22

the calling of Tychicus. In fact, Onesimus was a bonded slave and the property of Philemon. He was a new Christian and not yet equipped for ministry. It would appear that Tychicus was a mentor in the place of Paul who had brought Onesimus to Christ. In all these things, Tychicus epitomized the ministry of chaplaincy.

The chaplain's ministry of encouragement is most often directed toward those who have no immediate direct or organic association with the local church. In Acts chapter 9, we find such a ministry in connection with the conversion of Saul of Tarsus and the subsequent assistance of Ananias.

[10] Now there was a disciple at Damascus named Ananias. The Lord said to him in a vision, "Ananias." And he said, "Here I am, Lord." [11] And the Lord said to him, "Rise and go to the street called Straight, and at the house of Judas look for a man of Tarsus named Saul, for behold, he is praying, [12] and he has seen in a vision a man named Ananias come in and lay his hands on him so that he might regain his sight." [13] But Ananias answered, "Lord, I have heard from many about this man, how much evil he has done to your saints at Jerusalem. [14] And here he has authority from the chief priests to bind all who call on your name." [15] But the Lord said to him, "Go, for he is a chosen instrument of mine to carry my name before the Gentiles and kings and the children of Israel. [16] For I will show him how much he must suffer for the sake of my name." [17] So Ananias departed and entered the house. And laying his hands on him he said, "Brother Saul, the Lord Jesus who appeared to you on the road by which you came has sent me so that you may regain your sight and be filled with the Holy Spirit." [18] And immediately something like

scales fell from his eyes, and he regained his sight. Then he rose and was baptized; [19] and taking food, he was strengthened." Acts 9:10-19

Surely, at this point in his life, Saul was not only unaffiliated with a Christian church, but was, in fact, an enemy of the churches. Ananias was led to bring encouragement to a bewildered and broken Pharisee. Ananias was not without trepidation, nevertheless he went to Saul (a representative of the Jewish rulers) in Damascus and instructed him in the Lord Jesus and introduced him to the Holy Spirit. The result of the faithful witness of Ananias was the bringing of Saul to the disciples in Damascus where he would receive further instruction in Christianity. Ananias is another example of one who did the work that we associate with chaplaincy.

Probably the most significant New Testament example of the ministry of chaplaincy is found in the life of Philip the Evangelist. Philip was the second person chosen by the church in Jerusalem to serve when commissioned to do so by the Apostles. It is said that he was "of good repute, full of the Sprit and of wisdom." It is a familiar passage concerning the early days of the Church.

> Now in these days when the disciples were increasing in number, a complaint by the Hellenists arose against the Hebrews because their widows were being neglected in the daily distribution. [2] And the twelve summoned the full number of the disciples and said, "It is not right that we should give up preaching the word of God to serve tables. [3] Therefore, brothers, pick out from among you seven men of good repute, full of the Spirit and of wisdom, whom we will appoint to this duty. [4] But we will devote ourselves to prayer and to the ministry of the word." [5] And what

they said pleased the whole gathering, and they chose
Stephen, a man full of faith and of the Holy Spirit,
and Philip, and Prochorus, and Nicanor, and Timon,
and Parmenas, and Nicolaus, a proselyte of Antioch.
[6] These they set before the apostles, and they prayed
and laid their hands on them. [7] And the word of God
continued to increase, and the number of the disciples
multiplied greatly in Jerusalem, and a great many of
the priests became obedient to the faith." Acts 6:1-7

There are a number of interesting observations that can be
made concerning these men. They were the first deacons, but
it is clear that they enjoyed the commissioning of both the
church and the Apostles and some were ultimately appointed
to a more comprehensive ministry than that of the modern day
deacon. "They (the church and the apostles) laid their hands on
them," suggesting ordination. At least partially, as a result of
their commission "the word of God continued to increase... the
number of the disciples multiplied greatly," and "a great many
of the priests" were saved.

Stephen (apparently the first selected) went on to become
the first recorded Christian martyr. He was a powerful preacher.
Acts 6:8 reveals that he "did great wonders and miracles among
the people. Verse 10 goes on to say that the people "could
not withstand the wisdom and the Spirit with which he was
speaking." His ministry was so authoritative that they "stopped
their ears and rushed together at him."[49]

The second person selected in that group of godly men
was Philip. Though he was ordained and supervised by the
church, he was led of the Holy Spirit to travel to the city of
Samaria where he began to preach Christ. He, too, had a powerful
and effective ministry. He encountered several challenges from
the secular culture including an encounter with a sorcerer who
recognized the validity of Philip's ministry. The Holy Spirit

49 Acts 7:57,58

directed Philip farther South into the Gaza desert, where he met up with a government official from Ethiopia. Police chaplains would equate his experience with the Ethiopian eunuch as History's first "ride-along." The story is told in Acts 8:27-39.

"[27] And he [Philip] rose and went. And there was an Ethiopian, a eunuch, a court official of Candace, queen of the Ethiopians, who was in charge of all her treasure. He had come to Jerusalem to worship [28] and was returning, seated in his chariot, and he was reading the prophet Isaiah. [29] And the Spirit said to Philip, "Go over and join this chariot." [30] So Philip ran to him and heard him reading Isaiah the prophet and asked, "Do you understand what you are reading?" [31] And he said, "How can I, unless someone guides me?" And he invited Philip to come up and sit with him. [32] Now the passage of the Scripture that he was reading was this:

'Like a sheep he was led to the slaughter and like a lamb before its shearer is silent, so he opens not his mouth. [33] *In his humiliation justice was denied him. Who can describe his generation? For his life is taken away from the earth.'*

[34] And the eunuch said to Philip, "About whom, I ask you, does the prophet say this, about himself or about someone else?" [35] Then Philip opened his mouth, and beginning with this Scripture he told him the good news about Jesus. [36] And as they were going along the road they came to some water, and the eunuch said, "See, here is water! What prevents me from being baptized?" [38] And he commanded the chariot to stop, and they both went down into the water, Philip and the eunuch, and he baptized him. [39] And when

they came up out of the water, the Spirit of the Lord
carried Philip away, and the eunuch saw him no more,
and went on his way rejoicing."

Philip was a godly man; filled with the Holy Spirit and wisdom;
an accomplished preacher; an effective witness; and a chaplain
who ministered beyond the boundaries, but within the discipline
of the church.

Philip was the servant who was chosen by God to
minister in Samaria. There was no church there, as yet, and
the Jewish Christians would have looked upon Samaria as a
region where there was little orthodox religion. There is no
evidence that he established a church there, as would have
been the case with a missionary (New Testament evangelist),
in fact when the church in Jerusalem heard of Philip's ministry
there they sent Peter and John to pray with the converts and
instruct them more thoroughly.[50] Apparently, the church in
Jerusalem continued to oversee Philip's ministry. The fact that
Philip was baptizing coupled with the realization that baptism
is an ordinance given to the church (not the minister) would
also testify of this oversight.

In Gaza he encouraged the Ethiopian official. From
there, he went to Azotus, a Philistine city which Caesar (the
civil authority) had given to Herod. Again, he is ministering in
a location that is somewhat remote from the church that sent
him and where he would be required to minister in a secular
venue. Finally, we find him in Caesarea, sixty-two miles from
his home church, a city built by King Herod and named for
the Roman Emperor Caesar Augustus. It was another location
associated with the civil government and so we again find Philip
ministering among those we would term *the un-churched*. His
was not the usual parish ministry, but a vital one.

Some years later we find him still in Caesarea where he has
become known as the evangelist and there he entertains Paul and

---

50 Acts 8:14

his company on their way to Jerusalem.[51] His activity is a biblical example of ministry that resembles both Christian chaplaincy and, later, the more specific work of an evangelist (church planter)[52] reminiscent of today's pastor/chaplain. It is abundantly clear that he was the recipient of a divine call and the leading of the Holy Spirit; and it was so recognized by the church.

Tychicus and Philip join the list of biblical portrayals of men who were called of God to a ministry comprising that which we would identify with chaplaincy. In each instance, we can categorize their activities as New Testament examples of divine appointment to ministry with the oversight of the local church. We conclude, then, that chaplaincy is seen in the early church as an authentic ministry demonstrating a *bona fide* commission from God recognized by the local church. There is little question of this pattern when we consider the military chaplain, who is required by his endorsing church or denomination to provide evidence of his calling, and the endorsement itself is substantiation of the confidence and oversight of the church. This pattern is also clear in modern day chaplaincies in which much of what we understand as chaplaincy is performed by pastors who have a primary responsibility of shepherding a local church. The issue is less clear when we consider that unpaid volunteers who must seek remuneration in secular employment provide much of the chaplain ministry in community service, corporate and organizational venues. Though there is no biblical example of a divine calling that is unique solely to chaplaincy, it is quite reasonable to understand that there is a call of God into ministry and chaplaincy is a notable component of clergical pursuit. Hopefully, this study will provide encouragement in identifying those who are thus divinely called to ministry and led into chaplaincy.

The divine calling of God into ministry (be it pastoral, missionary, chaplaincy or other) can be demonstrated by a

---

51 Acts 21:8

52 It is the conviction of the author that a New Testament evangelist was what we today call a church planter, but that will be left for another time.

biblical pattern that is evident in the early church. In fact, it is illustrated somewhat in the same process that God uses to bring us to faith in Christ. Writing to the church in Rome, Paul addressed his letter to "all those in Rome who are loved by God and *called to be saints*;..."[53] (emphasis mine). Again, the church in Corinth is reminded that they "are sanctified in Christ Jesus, *called to be saints*, together with all those who in every place call upon the name of our Lord Jesus Christ..."[54] [emphasis mine]. Every true believer is the recipient of a call to salvation. In John 6:44, the Lord Jesus made it clear that "No one can come to me, unless the father who sent me draws him..." We are all "strangers to the covenants of promise"[55] until that call brings us to Christ. "For the promise is for you, and for your children, and for all who are far off, everyone whom the Lord our God calls to himself."[56] "And those whom he predestined he also called, and those whom he called he also justified, and those whom he justified he also glorified."[57] There is a divine call that delivers from the death of sin to the life of Christ. If God chooses to call us to Himself for salvation, does He not also exercise His sovereignty in calling some to a divinely appointed ministry? It would be foolish to think otherwise.

In Romans 1:1, Paul identified himself as one who was "called to be an apostle, set apart for the gospel of God." Again, in 1 Corinthians 1:1, he insisted that he was "called by the will of God to be an apostle of Christ Jesus." These two references are clear evidence of a distinct divine call to ministry for two reasons: First, it is clear that Paul's call to ministry was not the result of the will of man, but of the will of God. Second, he spoke of his call to ministry in close proximity to the general call to salvation, thereby identifying the call to ministry as distinct from the call to salvation extended to all true believers.

---

53 Romans 1:7
54 1 Corinthians 1:2
55 Ephesians 2:12
56 Acts 2:39
57 Romans 8:30

The Apostle had both calls in mind when confirming them to the church in Galatia. "...He who had set me apart before I was born and who called me by his grace, was pleased to reveal his Son to me, in order that I might preach him among the Gentiles...."[58] Further light is shed on the distinction of Paul's calling into ministry in Acts 20:24 where he referenced it saying, "But I do not account my life of any value nor as precious to myself, if only I may finish my course and the ministry that I received from the Lord Jesus, to testify to the gospel of the grace of God." His desire was to finish two overwhelmingly valuable objectives. The first of these was his "course" (δρόμος – dromos, literally, *a place for running*). In 2 Timothy 4:7, the same word is employed to refer to the race of faith. "...I have finished the race, I have kept the faith..." The second objective is to finish "the ministry that I received from the Lord Jesus..." Ministry, here, is διακονία [diakonia] which refers to serving. We can be confident in understanding these to be distinct calls inasmuch as dromos [course] is a masculine noun and diakonia (ministry) is a feminine noun. They must necessarily refer to distinct objectives.

This vocational calling was not unique to Paul. Writing to Timothy who was pastor-teacher of the church in Ephesus, he reminded him to "walk in a manner worthy of the calling to which you have been called..."[59] The King James version renders Timothy's calling his "vocation," emphasizing the uniqueness of Timothy's charge. The verb form of the word is employed by the Holy Spirit in Hebrews 11:8 to describe the commissioning of Abraham "when he was called to go out to a place that he was to receive as an inheritance...."

We must be careful to avoid reading into these passages an exalted class of individual that we term clergy and a second, larger grouping called laity. There is no biblical support for

---

58   Galatians 1:15
59   Ephesians 4:1

that view. Scripture makes it abundantly clear that every true believer is at once a saint, and a priest before God. The apostles Paul, Peter and John all make this abundantly clear:

> "To all those in Rome who are loved by God and *called to be saints...*" Romans 1:7

> "To the church of God that is in Corinth, to those sanctified in Christ Jesus, *called to be saints together with all those who in every place call upon the name of our Lord Jesus Christ*, both their Lord and ours." 1 Corinthians 1:2[60]

> "...you yourselves like living stones are being built up as a spiritual house, *to be a holy priesthood*, to offer spiritual sacrifices acceptable to God through Jesus Christ." 1 Peter 2:5

> "But you are a chosen race, *a royal priesthood*, a holy nation, a people for his own possession, that you may proclaim the excellencies of him who called you out of darkness into his marvelous light." 1 Peter 2:9

> "To him who loves us and has freed us from our sins by his blood and made us a kingdom, *priests to his God and Father*, to him be glory and dominion forever and ever. Amen." Revelation 1:5b- 6 (*Emphasis mine*)

Rather, we ought to understand that God has exercised His sovereignty, not only in the call to salvation, but also to those whom He has appointed to specific tasks for His own purpose and glory. We are saved by the sovereign will of God as those "who were born, not of blood, nor of the will of the flesh, nor of

---

60   See also 2 Corinthians 1:1; Ephesians 1:1; Philippians 1:1; Colossians 1:2, 12; Jude 3

the will of man, but of God."[61] Is it any surprise, then, that He exercise His will in the matter of ministry?

How then does one determine whether his desire to enter a vocational (divinely appointed) ministry is a genuine call of God? Does GPC mean "Go preach Christ," or "Go plow corn?" It is not sufficient merely to desire the position. The simple emotional desire is always an inadequate barometer, especially when confronted with the many difficulties of ministry, and the fallacy of which is so often demonstrated in the heartbreak of a discredited ministry. Might the tragedy of chaplains who have fallen by the wayside in defeat and disgrace have been avoided by a more careful understanding and evaluation of the call of God at the outset? Surely, there must be some objective revealed biblical truth that can guide us in this important consideration.

Nor is providence alone a sufficient indicator of the will of God. Time and again we have heard the testimony of a candidate for chaplaincy (or some other venue of ministry) that relied entirely on some set of apparently significant circumstances not unlike the sign in the sky illustration with which we began this chapter. One such person was convinced she was called to chaplaincy, because she was contemplating what to do while driving and stopped at a traffic signal beside another vehicle that was marked "CHAPLAIN." The suggestion was so strong that she concluded she had experienced the call of God. Even a cursory study of scripture would have shown that individual was not biblically suited for ministry, but biblical criteria were never considered. To be sure, God's will is accomplished in every unfolding of reality, but there is no way to know of a certainty whether a particular event is intended to direct one in a particular path. An interesting sidelight of Paul's journey to Rome illustrates this truth rather forcefully.

---

61 John 1:13

³ When Paul had gathered a bundle of sticks and put them on the fire, a viper came out because of the heat and fastened on his hand. ⁴ When the native people saw the creature hanging from his hand, they said to one another, "No doubt this man is a murderer. Though he has escaped from the sea, Justice has not allowed him to live." ⁵ He, however, shook off the creature into the fire and suffered no harm. ⁶ They were waiting for him to swell up or suddenly fall down dead. But when they had waited a long time and saw no misfortune come to him, they changed their minds and said that he was a god. Acts 28:3-6

Those who witnessed this event drew two different conclusions of its meaning. First they saw in the strike of the viper confirmation of Paul's guilt. They thought him to be a murderer receiving his just desserts. When their expectations were not realized, they saw him as a god. Both conclusions were very wrong. Some to this day have foolishly read into this passage a justification for employing poisonous snakes in their worship. It was a popular conception among the Jews that misfortune in a person's life must necessarily be an indicator of sin. In John 9:1-3, the Lord addressed that fallacy. "As he passed, he saw a man blind from birth. And his disciples asked him, 'Rabbi, who sinned, this man or his parents, that he was born blind?' Jesus answered, 'It was not that this man sinned, or his parents, but that the works of God might be displayed in him." It is evident that even tragedy can take place for no other reason than to point to the works and glory of God. Certainly, it is true that misfortune will often come as a result of sin, but without some clear proclamation of scripture to that effect, we should not automatically draw that conclusion. If a chaplain confuses his call only with some sort of remarkable circumstance, how will he explain the glory of God to the recipient of tragedy and sorrow?

If a mother loses her infant child from sudden infant death syndrome, is she to assume that she is being punished? And if a thief prospers financially through his dishonest dealings, is he to draw satisfaction from the blessing of God? Yet God has His own purpose in both events. We should always remember that Satan also brings about circumstances that may be interpreted in deceptive ways.

That is not to say that God does not bring meaningful experience into the lives of those He is preparing for specific ministry to equip them for future service, which may not be understood until God is ready to employ it. Particularly in chaplaincy, I think, it is likely that He may well call out those who are able to share in some fashion the experience of those to whom they minister. Paul's background as a member of the Jewish Sanhedrin was a fitting preparation for his subsequent ministry. It is interesting to note that though it was Paul, who was called to be an Apostle to the Gentiles, it was his understanding of the Jewish laws and customs that providentially led to his journey to Rome and a fruitful ministry among the Gentiles there. No doubt Peter's failure during the trial of Christ was a valuable reminder in his subsequent ministry. One wonders if it was in his mind when he insisted "If you are insulted for the name of Christ, you are blessed, because the Spirit of glory and of God rests upon you…"[62] Nothing has entered the life of the believer that has not been filtered through the will of God.

The need for chaplaincy (or ministry of any sort) is not a sufficient indicator of a call. There are needs all about us and we tend to be selective about those to which we respond. There are more needs than we could possibly address. The mission field beckons from every corner of the earth where millions languish in sin and ignorance of the Gospel. It would be unusual to find any people group or social composition where a gospel witness is not needed. It has always been my understanding that when a believer sees a need and is equipped to address it, he should do

---

62   1 Peter 4:14

so unless God closes the door, but that is far from interpreting the need as a heavenly call to a divinely appointed ministry. Certainly, it is not necessary to obtain ordination to minister to one another. We have already established that Christians are both kings and priests. Galatians 6:10 insists "as we have opportunity, let us do good to everyone, and especially to those who are of the household of faith." An appeal based only on need denigrates the sovereignty of God, because it does not recognize the work of God in opening and closing doors of ministry, not does it consider similar indicators that may have satanic origin.

Ability is not a profound indicator of a call to a divinely appointed ministry. 1 Corinthians 1:26-29 reminds us to "Consider your calling, brothers: not many of you were wise according to worldly standards, not many were powerful, not many were of noble birth. But God chose what is low and despised in the world, even things that are not, to bring to nothing things that are, so that no human being might boast in the presence of God." The Apostle Paul, speaking of his call to ministry, affirmed that he was "the very least of all the saints,"[63] and the foremost of sinners.[64] God has chosen to use many an unimpressive vessel that was not esteemed in the world to bring about wondrous works. It was said of Paul: "His letters are weighty and strong, but his bodily presence is weak, and his speech of no account."[65]

So then, how is one to know if he is constrained by the call of God to a divinely appointed ministry? There is a New Testament pattern that merits our consideration. In First Corinthians chapter 9, Paul spoke of his call and that of Barnabas. He drew a comparison to the priests of old who were appointed to care for the temple, reminding the Corinthians that he had not demanded of them those material remunerations

---

63 Ephesians 3:8
64 1 Timothy 1:15
65 2 Corinthians 10:10

to which he was entitled as an Apostle. In verses sixteen and seventeen he insisted: For if I preach the gospel, that gives me no ground for boasting. For necessity is laid upon me. Woe to me if I do not preach the gospel! For if I do this of my own will, I have a reward, but if not of my own will, I am still entrusted with a stewardship." A true calling from God into ministry is a divine charge that must not be ignored. It is not the product of personal desire, human providence, need or ability, though all of these things may be present, nor is it an option. It is a sovereign decree of God, compelling the recipient to follow the course laid out by God. But how is one to know what is God's leading and what is simply subjective impression? One cannot expect to have the experience of Paul who was struck down on the road to Damascus, confronted by the risen Christ and given a specific verbal instruction. That occurrence was necessitated by the absence of a written New Testament revelation. We must look to the more objective standard of scripture to recognize God's divine appointment to ministry.

A classic biblical example of a draft to ministry is found in the testimony of Isaiah:

> "In the year that King Uzziah died I saw the Lord sitting upon a throne, high and lifted up; and the train of his robe filled the temple. ² Above him stood the seraphim. Each had six wings: with two he covered his face, and with two he covered his feet, and with two he flew. ³ And one called to another and said:
>
> *'Holy, holy, holy is the LORD of hosts; the whole earth is full of his glory!'*
>
> ⁴ And the foundations of the thresholds shook at the voice of him who called, and the house was filled with smoke. ⁵ And I said: "Woe is me! For I am lost; for I am a man of unclean lips, and I dwell in the midst of a people of unclean lips; for my eyes have seen the King, the LORD of hosts!"

⁶ Then one of the seraphim flew to me, having in his hand a burning coal that he had taken with tongs from the altar. ⁷ And he touched my mouth and said: *'Behold, this has touched your lips; your guilt is taken away, and your sin atoned for.'*

⁸ And I heard the voice of the Lord saying, *'Whom shall I send, and who will go for us?'* Then I said, *'Here am I! Send me.'"* Isaiah 6:1-8

Isaiah was struck with a vision of the uniqueness of God even to the point of despair. He was struck by a vision of the Lord in His glory. He was broken by the realization of his sin and in abject humility was driven to confession – prostrate before God. There was no thought of honor or recognition or standing, except for the realization that he had none. In this instance there was no sense of exaltation, rather the reality of his sin.

The first requisite for recognizing God's divine call to ministry is an awareness of the glory of God and the conviction of our own sin. John the Baptist expressed it this way: "He must increase, but I must decrease."[66] Ministry is not about the aspirant, it's about the Almighty; it's not about the honor, it's about the Holy One; it's not about the accolades, it's about the Advocate; it's not about the vestments of the church, it's about the vicarious death of Christ; it's not about the title of the minister, it's about the task of the Mediator; its not about the recognition of the crowd, its about the redemption of the cross; it's not about the gift of gab, it's about the glory of God. I once asked a cleric who was about to retire why he chose ministry and would he do it again. His answer astonished me. "When I was a boy I was not very well thought of," he said, "so I wanted an occupation that would give me respect." "Go plow corn," I thought. It is unfortunately true that there is no shortage of those who choose chaplaincy as a means to gain

---

[66] John 3:30

validation as a minister. In terms of a divine call into ministry, those need not apply. Paul's question, "Who are you, Lord?"[67] was an expression of wonderment not unlike that of Isaiah; a complete and unconditional surrender to the lordship of Christ.

The second essential consideration of the validity of a call to ministry is recognition of the testimony and gifts of the candidate by the church. This New Testament pattern is illustrated in Acts 6:1-4.

> Now in these days when the disciples were increasing in number, a complaint by the Hellenists arose against the Hebrews because their widows were being neglected in the daily distribution. [2] And the twelve summoned the full number of the disciples and said, "It is not right that we should give up preaching the word of God to serve tables. [3] Therefore, brothers, pick out from among you seven men of good repute, full of the Spirit and of wisdom, whom we will appoint to this duty. [4] But we will devote ourselves to prayer and to the ministry of the word.

Though this passage deals with the calling of the first deacons, we have already seen that at least some of these men were appointed ministry that extended well beyond the task of caring for the Hellenic widows. We must be careful to assign their duty to the widows the significant biblical prominence it deserves. The Apostle James made it clear that "Religion that is pure and undefiled before God, the Father, is this: to visit orphans and widows in their affliction, and to keep oneself unstained from the world."[68] These are, notably, distinctive activities associated with the early deacons and often today (in a practical sense) of a chaplain.

---

67 Acts 9:5

68 James 1:27

The recognition and recommendation of the church is essential, because the candidate for ministry must have consistently demonstrated the characteristics of a mature Christian testimony. If even the apostles found it wise to consult with the church (those who were in the best position to know the life and testimony of the ones who were considered) does it not commend the same process to us? Matthew Henry put it this way:

> They *called the multitude of the disciples unto them*, the heads of the congregations of Christians in Jerusalem, the principal leading men. The twelve themselves would not determine any thing without them, for *in multitude of counselors there is safety;* and in an affair of this nature those might be best able to advise who were more conversant in the affairs of this life than the apostles were."[69]

They sought men who were "of good repute, full of the spirit and of wisdom."[70] Who better able to offer such an evaluation than the folks with whom the candidates lived and worshipped on a regular basis? And if such an assessment is found necessary for the office of deacon, should it not also encompass the consideration of a chaplain, and certainly a bishop/pastor/elder?

The first concern of the Apostles was that these men be "of good repute." The word employed is μαρτυρουμένους [martyroumenous] from a word meaning to bear witness (μαρτυρέω). Interestingly, it is the word from which we get the English word martyr. It was of note that those considered for ministry were to have a good witness where they were and assurance was demanded that their witness was true and reliable. In other words, they were expected to have a firm understanding

---

69   Henry, Matthew. (1996, c1991). *Matthew Henry's Commentary on the Whole Bible :* Complete and unabridged in one volume (Ac 6:1). Peabody: Hendrickson.

70   Acts 6:3

of the Gospel and they were to be consistent in their proclamation of it by both life and lip. The same word is used in Acts 26:22, 23 (rendered "testifying") when Paul witnessed to King Agrippa saying "I have had the help that comes from God, and so I stand here **testifying** both to small and great, saying nothing but what the prophets and Moses said would come to pass: that the Christ must suffer and that, by being the first to rise from the dead, he would proclaim light both to our people and to the Gentiles." [Emphasis mine] The declaration of Paul was that his testimony was consistent to everyone, and was focused on the Word of God as it pertained to the Lord Jesus Christ. In the balance, Paul was found to be "of good repute." No less was expected of the early deacons and no less should be characteristic of a call to ministry. If one finds boldness to witness only *after* seeking appointment to chaplaincy, there is overpowering reason to question the validity of the call.

The next consideration was that they be filled with the Holy Spirit. Ephesians 5:18 acquaints us with both the definition and the necessity of this requirement: "And do not get drunk with wine, for that is debauchery, but be filled with the Spirit." We must first ask what it means to be "filled with the Spirit," for there is no small amount of misunderstanding of the topic. Though some have taught that a believer is blessed with a second work of grace whereby he or she is given a greater measure of the Holy Spirit, thereby achieving a higher plane of sanctification, there is no scriptural basis for that view. When a person is saved, he or she is permanently indwelled by the Holy Spirit and baptized into the body of Christ.[71] What then, does it mean to be filled with the Spirit? The renowned Greek scholar Kenneth Wuest makes a compelling case for understanding the construction of the verb and noun in this statement to refer to the Holy Spirit's control of the believer. He follows his grammatical argument with this observation:

---

71 1 Corinthians 12:13

"We must not think of the Holy Spirit filling our hearts as water fills a bottle, or air, a vacuum, or a bushel of oats, an empty basket. The heart of a Christian is not a receptacle to be emptied in order that the Holy Spirit might fill it. The Holy Spirit is not a substance to fill an empty receptacle, He is a Person to control another person, the believer. He does not fill a Christian's life with Himself. He controls that person."[72]

Being "filled with the Spirit," has nothing to do with how much of the Spirit is possessed by the believer, but has everything to do with how much the believer is possessed by the Spirit. Hence, the reference to the inebriation brought about by excess wine.

What might the church observe and testify of the life of someone who is filled with the Holy Spirit? Our thoughts go immediately to Galatians 5:22, 23 where the "fruit of the Spirit is clearly outlined: "But the fruit of the Spirit is love, joy, peace, patience, kindness, goodness, faithfulness, gentleness, self-control; against such things there is no law." The local church is in the best position to attest to the fruit of the Spirit in the life of its members. It is an appropriate consideration for ministry in view of the assertion of Ephesians 5:9-10: "For the fruit of the Spirit is in all goodness and righteousness and truth; *Proving what is acceptable unto the Lord.*" (KJV) [Emphasis mine]

A third indication of fitness for ministry of which the church was asked to attest is wisdom. Proverbs 4:7 (KJV) insists "Wisdom is the principal thing; therefore get wisdom...." In scripture, wisdom is associated with a respect for God. "The fear of the LORD is the beginning of wisdom...."[73] Solomon was given a measure of wisdom above all his peers. 2 Chronicles 9:23 says of him: "And all the kings of the earth sought the presence of Solomon, to hear his wisdom, which God had put

---

72 Kenneth S. Wuest, Untranslatable Riches From The Greek New Testament, Wm. B, Eerdmans Publishing Company, Grand Rapids, MI, 1942, page 104

73 Psalm 111:10

in his mind." It is of note that God gave such extraordinary wisdom to Solomon when he asked for discernment between good and evil.

> [5] At Gibeon the LORD appeared to Solomon in a dream by night, and God said, "Ask what I shall give you." [6] And Solomon said, "You have shown great and steadfast love to your servant David my father, because he walked before you in faithfulness, in righteousness, and in uprightness of heart toward you. And you have kept for him this great and steadfast love and have given him a son to sit on his throne this day. [7] And now, O LORD my God, you have made your servant king in place of David my father, although I am but a little child. I do not know how to go out or come in. [8] And your servant is in the midst of your people whom you have chosen, a great people, too many to be numbered or counted for multitude. [9] Give your servant therefore an understanding mind to govern your people, that I may discern between good and evil, for who is able to govern this your great people?"
> [10] It pleased the Lord that Solomon had asked this. [11] And God said to him, "Because you have asked this, and have not asked for yourself long life or riches or the life of your enemies, but have asked for yourself understanding to discern what is right, [12] behold, I now do according to your word. Behold, I give you a wise and discerning mind, so that none like you has been before you and none like you shall arise after you. 1 Kings 3:5-12

Solomon wanted to know what to do and how to choose between right and wrong. He would later write "whatever you get,

get insight."[74] Seventy-seven times in the bible, wisdom and understanding are linked together in the same verse. Forty-six times in the bible, wisdom and knowledge are linked together in one verse. Deuteronomy 4:5, 6 equates wisdom with keeping the statutes and judgments of God:

> [5] See, I have taught you statutes and rules, as the LORD my God commanded me, that you should do them in the land that you are entering to take possession of it. [6] Keep them and do them, for *that will be your wisdom and your understanding* in the sight of the peoples, who, when they hear all these statutes, will say, 'Surely this great nation is a wise and understanding people. [Emphasis mine]

Putting these biblical descriptions together, we arrive at a working definition of wisdom. Wisdom is the ability to discern that right course of action which is always consistent with the will of God. Essentially, it is knowledge of what to do that is pleasing to God. It is a fundamental quality for ministry. The church would know whether a candidate was wise in his deportment or was prone to make decisions that hindered spiritual growth. The church in Jerusalem made a wise choice in their recognition of these seven men. Just a short time later, it is said of the ministry of the first of those selected that those who opposed the Gospel "could not withstand the wisdom and the Spirit with which he was speaking."[75]

It is of note that when ministry was needed, the Apostles did not ask for volunteers, but rather relied on the church's recognition of the gifts and suitability for ministry of its members. We see here, also, an early indication of the congregational polity of the early church. "And what they said pleased the whole gathering, and they chose...."[76] Without the

---

74 Proverbs 4:7b

75 Acts 6:10

76 Acts 6:5

confidence of the church, a candidate for chaplaincy will be left adrift and his compass will surely waver.

A third biblical factor in recognizing a divine call is the willingness of a church to extend ordination. Following the validation of gifts fitting the candidates for ministry, the church affixed its seal of confidence and oversight upon those who were chosen. After consideration and prayer, they "laid their hands on them,"[77] suggesting what we today call ordination. The term is somewhat vague, but no more so than the contemporary practice. In a time when the *Every Day Church of the What's Happening Now* markets ordination certificates online and even some churches are willing to "ordain" members and friends simply for the asking, this important practice has lost some credibility. But proper ordination by a church represents not only the recommendation of the aspirant, but also the responsibility to oversee the minister's life and ministry. The reader must not equate the ordination of which we speak with that of some para-church organizations that provide credentials apart from the examination and endorsement of a local church. There is no biblical support for this practice, which has encouraged many candidates for chaplaincy to shop endorsers until finding someone willing to "ordain" them, even though their own church may be reluctant to do so.

Shopping endorsers is a particularly onerous problem in chaplaincy, which typically requires the applicant to obtain an endorsement from a religious body before a chaplain appointment is granted. This unfortunate loophole persists, because government agencies, in particular, are reluctant, on constitutional grounds, to question the credibility of a chaplain's endorsement. In the New Testament pattern, the church is the only institution with the biblical authority to ordain, as we will demonstrate in a subsequent chapter of this treatise. What validity can there be for endorsement to ministry on the part of those who have not consistently witnessed the

---

77 Acts 6:6

life and testimony of the prospective chaplain and evaluated his suitability and call to ministry? Surely, it cannot be done by an agency or organization that performs such examination online or through advertising for those who wish to become chaplains. One cannot conclude that all chaplains who are ordained outside the church are otherwise unqualified or inadequate for the job, but the case can be made that they lack the biblical oversight of a local church.

A fourth consideration is closely related to the New Testament concept of ordination, but warrants its own explanation. The commissioning of the minister by the church flows from and naturally follows the confirmation of the aspirant's call and the consecration evidenced by ordination. They are so closely related they might be considered two aspects of a consecration to ministry – ordination and oversight demonstrated in Acts 13:1-3. The ordination of Paul and Barnabas was followed by the commissioning of the church.

> Now there were in the church at Antioch prophets and teachers, Barnabas, Simeon who was called Niger, Lucius of Cyrene, Manaen a member of the court of Herod the tetrarch, and Saul. [2] While they were worshiping the Lord and fasting, the Holy Spirit said, "Set apart for me Barnabas and Saul for the work to which I have called them." [3] Then after fasting and praying they laid their hands on them and sent them off.

In Acts chapter six it was the Apostles that sought the endorsement of the church, no doubt as directed by the Holy Spirit. It is of note that even the Apostles were expected to consult the authority of the church. In Acts chapter thirteen, the Holy Spirit Himself presented the church with the same responsibility. Acts 13:4 tells us that Barnabas and Saul were "sent out by the Holy Spirit," but it must not go without notice that their sending involved the direction of the Holy Spirit, followed by confirmation, consecration and commissioning on the part of the local church. It was a thoughtful consideration, evidenced by the revelation their action was preceded by fasting and prayer. Commissioning is yet another indication of the oversight of the church. Up until this time Saul, apparently, was a preacher in training, but now he is set apart with Barnabas for specific ministry. The confidence of ordination was bestowed upon them and they were sent away (commissioned by the church) for the work to which the Holy Spirit had called them.

There is a godly desire to enter Gospel ministry. Paul reminded Timothy "If anyone aspires to the office of overseer [bishop], he desires a noble task."[78] Immediately; however, he spoke of the requisite in terms of a life that is wholly given over to God.[79] The desire for vocational (divinely appointed) ministry must be tempered by an understanding of the cost of discipleship and validation of its authenticity by the church. Perhaps Paul's advice to Timothy was a response to those in the church in Ephesus who desired the office, but fell short of the commitment. There has never been a shortage of those who desired the office, but care must always be exercised to seek the guidance of the church.

A God-sent call to vocational ministry will always conform to the context and declaration of scripture. As we have already seen, it is the Holy Spirit that calls in Acts 13:1-3, and living under the control of the Holy Spirit is a requisite for ministry according to the expectations of Acts 6:3. In Acts 16:6-10 we find the Holy Spirit active in directing Paul to specific venues of ministry:

> [6] And they went through the region of Phrygia and Galatia, having been forbidden by the Holy Spirit to speak the word in Asia. [7] And when they had come

---

78   1 Timothy 3:1
79   1 Timothy 3:2-7

up to Mysia, they attempted to go into Bithynia, but the Spirit of Jesus did not allow them. [8] So, passing by Mysia, they went down to Troas. [9] And a vision appeared to Paul in the night: a man of Macedonia was standing there, urging him and saying, "Come over to Macedonia and help us." [10] And when Paul had seen the vision, immediately we sought to go on into Macedonia, concluding that God had called us to preach the gospel to them.

Some may object to the suggestion that the local church bears the responsibility for the oversight of ministry, insisting they are led only by the Holy Spirit, and not subject to a church. This concern will be addressed in chapter four where we will take up the biblical basis for church oversight of the minister subsequent to his calling, consecration and commissioning. It is self evident; however, that the Holy Spirit, Who is after all the author of scripture, would not lead someone contrary to that same scripture. "For no prophecy was ever produced by the will of man, but men spoke from God as they were carried along by the Holy Spirit."[80] Likewise, it is the Holy Spirit that teaches and guides us in prayer. "Likewise, the Spirit helps us in our weakness. For we do not know what to pray for as we ought, but the Spirit himself intercedes for us with groanings too deep for words. And he who searches hearts knows what is the mind of the Spirit, because the Spirit intercedes for the saints according to the will of God."[81]

It is inconceivable that God would contradict Himself. The Holy Spirit will not direct someone to ministry contrary to the biblical direction, which He also provided. It is foolish to espouse a "call" to ministry absent biblically defined criteria known to the familiar local church, and then argue its validity only by insisting "I prayed about it and am being led by the Holy

80 2 Peter 1:21
81 Romans 8:26, 27

Spirit." If it is contrary to scripture one may safely conclude it does not come from the Holy Spirit, for it is scripture that provides that "the man of God may be competent, equipped for every good work."[82] One should first examine whether the desire conforms to the Word of God, and if not, discard it as a suggestion from the flesh.

If, on the other hand, we are persuaded of a call from God; the church, in recognition of our gifts, encourages our progress; and both our life and prospective ministry are consistent with the Word of God and under the control of the Holy Spirit; we may be confident of such a calling.

---

82   2 Timothy 3:16, 17

CHAPTER FOUR

THE CHAPLAIN AND THE CHURCH

It had become somewhat of a familiar story. The voice on the other end of the telephone line was sincere and pleasant. *"I called,"* he said, *"to inquire into becoming a chaplain."*

The conversation went something like this:

"My name is Grant" [not his real name]. *"I met you at the prayer breakfast last week and I was very impressed with the work of the chaplaincy. I believe I have something to offer. I was a first responder for fifteen years and I have seen it all. I've been able to help a lot of people in crisis and several have sought me out for counsel. I'm a born again Christian and have studied the Bible for many years."*

"I appreciate your interest, Grant," was the cautious reply. *"How did you learn about our agency?"*

"Well, I heard you speak at the prayer breakfast, but several of my friends had already told me about the chaplaincy. I have one good friend who was shot in a robbery and she told me how helpful your chaplains were. I can do that."

"Oh my, that must have been a very traumatic experience for your friend. What did she find most helpful in that circumstance?"

"Mostly," he said, *"she was thankful that someone was there to pray with her"*

"I'm pleased that someone was there for her. Tell me about your background, Grant, and how you came to be interested in chaplaincy?"

"Well, as I said, I have been a Christian for many years and God has used me to help many people. I love the Lord, and

I want to serve Him and help others at the same time. Just last week, I met with a couple at work that are having problems in their marriage and was able to help them see the root cause of their anger and I told them that if they would just trust the Lord together, He would heal their family. I believe that God has given me the gift of discernment and the ability to help people."

"That's interesting, Grant. On what do you base your understanding of your gifts and your desire to become a chaplain?"

"I have been teaching a Bible study for three years now and have helped a lot of people with their understanding of the Bible. God has been really good to me and has given me wisdom to understand the scripture. The Holy Spirit has been leading me toward a full-time ministry."

"That's impressive, Grant. Tell me about your church."

"I haven't really settled in to one church yet. I moved here four years ago and I just haven't found the ideal fellowship. For a while I attended The Happening Church, but most of the time, I hold a Bible study in my home for my family and some others who just want to learn the Bible. I grew up in a really strict church that didn't have very many young people, so I drifted away when I was in high school, but when I went to college I got involved with a Christian fellowship on the campus and re-dedicated my life to God. Since then, the Bible has been my rock and Jesus has led me all the way. I went to the Golgotha Cathedral Bible Institute for a semester and did some street preaching among the homeless. God really blessed that ministry. I started this Bible study just after I moved here and it's grown to over 20 people now. God has really blessed it. Sometimes we meet on Sunday, so it's hard to find the church that's right for me. There are lots of good churches in town and I've visited most of them."

A shocking conversation? The truly dreadful reality is the discovery that many Christians would not find it at all shocking that an apparently gifted individual who desired to help others with the impartation of biblical truth, a smathering of theological study, self-proclaimed leadership qualities and such a casual attitude toward the church would be found equipped for chaplaincy. In some agencies, Grant would have been snapped up and appointed as a chaplain with little, if any, consideration of the fact that there is absolutely no spiritual authority over his life and ministry. The most crucial problem facing chaplaincy today is the failure to engage the local church in the oversight of chaplains. This is a particularly important concern for, by definition, the chaplain most often ministers to those who are outside the church, or at least temporarily away from the influence of their local church. A chaplain must maintain a constant fellowship and submission to his church if he wishes to avoid the many pitfalls that await him on the shoals of ministry in a secular environment.

Some years ago, a survey was conducted in a police chaplaincy consisting of about twenty-five chaplains. Questions were asked concerning the relationship of the chaplains with their church or denomination. The startling results found that only about thirty percent of them ever reported their activities to their church or denomination. About seventy percent of the time, there was no real spiritual oversight with regard to their ministry in chaplaincy. As established earlier in this study, chaplain agencies are rarely in a position to provide the necessary spiritual supervision. The almost universal use of ministers and workers from different theological perspectives assures an environment in which the oversight of doctrinal issues is a near impossibility. Government and other secular agencies lack the expertise to delve into such matters. Some chaplaincies are conducted in an arena that is hostile to religious training. It may well be that no area of ministry functions without adequate spiritual oversight to the degree that is common in chaplaincy. Perhaps this unfortunate dilemma explains much of the moral and ethical failure in chaplaincy that we noted earlier. The biblical solution to this prevalent and persistent problem is the local church. God has ordained the church to exercise oversight of the believer's life and ministry and the proclamation of the Gospel throughout the world.

The Church is the only institution built by Christ. The Lord Jesus made that clear in Matthew 16:18 when He promised "I will build my church; and the gates of hell shall not prevail against it." But it is often treated today as though the church is an optional, perhaps even unneeded social experiment, and indeed, much of the expression of the so called seeker friendly and emergent movements would substantiate that impression. There is a general lack of respect for the establishment that Christ promised and for which He suffered and died. There has been a shift toward ministry that functions outside the church with little or no oversight by the church and little, if any, effort made to bring believers into the authority of a church. Those who envision a project that does not have the approval of the church can simply start a group of their own, appoint themselves a title, and put out their shingle, so to speak. Much of the time these ministries stem from a genuine burden for a spiritual or social need in some target population. One can hardly argue with the compassion, or minimize the good that may come of their eleemosynary intentions; however, Christians must take steps to insure that they are individually and corporately responsible to the church if they are to expect God's approval. Neither a board of directors, group of supporters, cadre of volunteers or corporate structure can fill the role of the church in the Kingdom of God. Christian workers would do well to remember the wisdom of the centurion in Luke 7:8 who confessed to Christ "I also am a man set under authority."

In First Corinthians chapter three, Paul chided the church in Corinth for their divisions and encouraged them to build on the established foundation of the church. It is a significant passage concerning the works of believers in the Kingdom and it underscores the importance of local church oversight for any Christian ministry.

⁴ For when one says, "I follow Paul," and another, "I follow Apollos," are you not being merely human?

⁵ What then is Apollos? What is Paul? Servants through whom you believed, as the Lord assigned to each. ⁶ I planted, Apollos watered, but God gave the growth. ⁷ So neither he who plants nor he who waters is anything, but only God who gives the growth. ⁸ He who plants and he who waters are one, and each will receive his wages according to his labor. ⁹ For we are God's fellow workers. You are God's field, God's building.

¹⁰ According to the grace of God given to me, like a skilled master builder I laid a foundation, and someone else is building upon it. Let each one take care how he builds upon it. ¹¹ For no one can lay a foundation other than that which is laid, which is Jesus Christ. ¹² Now if anyone builds on the foundation with gold, silver, precious stones, wood, hay, straw—— ¹³ each one's work will become manifest, for the Day will disclose it, because it will be revealed by fire, and the fire will test what sort of work each one has done. ¹⁴ If the work that anyone has built on the foundation survives, he will receive a reward. ¹⁵ If anyone's work is burned up, he will suffer loss, though he himself will be saved, but only as through fire.

¹⁶ Do you not know that you are God's temple and that God's Spirit dwells in you? ¹⁷ If anyone destroys God's temple, God will destroy him. For God's temple is holy, and you are that temple. 1 Corinthians 3:4-17

Paul had planted the church in Corinth and they were a gifted group of people. There was division among them; however, and they began to form into cliques. Some clung to the memory of Paul; some preferred the eloquent preaching of Apollos who followed Paul in the pulpit. The Apostle pointed out to them that both he and Apollos were simply ministers whom God had used to bring them the Gospel. It was God who brought about the increase in their number and their spiritual growth. It was God who granted them gifts for the edification of all. It was important that they understood that it was God's church and they were all simply fellow laborers with Him and they were all a part of the whole. Without doubt, Paul is here speaking of the local church. He went on to say that he had only laid the foundation of their assembly. Apollos had come after him and built on that foundation. Now each of the church members were adding to the same foundation. Paul went on to remind them that they should exercise care in how they built, for their work would be judged. The purpose of that judgment would be to test the validity of their efforts. That which was pleasing to God is likened to gold, jewels and precious stones. That which is displeasing to God is seen as wood, hay and straw. The trial would be by fire and that which was built in disobedience would be consumed by it. He hastened to remind them that he was not here speaking of their salvation. The judgment was not that great judgment at the White Throne of God. They would suffer the loss of their reward for works performed in disobedience, but their salvation was secure.

We must keep in mind that all the while Paul has been speaking of the church. That is important to remember, because without that understanding, the significance of the next remarkable statement will be lost. He said "Do you not know that you are God's temple and that God's Spirit dwells in you?" (v.16) There is a good deal of misunderstanding about this important question. It is commonly thought that Paul is informing the believers in Corinth, and subsequently those of us who are saved today, that the individual believer is indwelled by the Holy Spirit. The truth of that understanding is borne out in First Corinthians 6:19 where Paul insists "Do you not know that your body is a temple of the Holy Spirit within you, whom you have from God?" It is indisputably true that the individual believer is indwelled by the Holy Spirit and is therefore a temple of God. But, that is *not* what Paul is saying in First Corinthians 3:16. The temple in chapter three and the temple in chapter six are not synonymous.

In First Corinthians 3:16, the Holy Spirit employs a singular noun with a plural verb. "Do you not know that you [plural] are God's temple [singular]." The reference here is to a number of people who comprise a single temple – the local church. In First Corinthians 6:19, the Holy Spirit employs both a singular noun and singular verb to say that the individual body of each believer is also a temple of the Holy Spirit, because each body is indwelled by the Holy Spirit. The reference in chapter three is to the corporate body of the church and the reference in chapter six is to the individual physical body of the believer. In chapter three, the temple is the church body. It is an understanding not unlike that in First Corinthians 12:27, "Now you are the body of Christ and individually members of it." Again, we find the grammatical structure of a plural verb used with a singular noun. In chapter six, the temples are the believer's bodies. Both are an essential part of understanding our relationship with Christ and with each other as members of His body.

With this understanding of Paul's instruction to the local church body as a temple of God, we can shed light on the significance of his declaration to the members of the church in Corinth. "If anyone destroys God's temple, God will destroy him. For God's temple is holy and you are that temple."[83] This admonition is not addressed to unbelievers who may wish to bring calamity upon the church. It is directed to members of the church who, are "behaving only in a human way" (v.3) by their divisive and dismissive works that are placing their own desires before the edification and oversight of the church. These works

---

83   1 Corinthians 3:17

will become manifest in the crucible of fire, and those that are not founded in the edification and authority of the local church will go up in flame. It is a serious thing to bring dissention or otherwise cause destruction in the church. The warning here is to take heed that what you do builds up the church. The word twice rendered destroy [φθείρω – phtheiro] in this verse means *to, corrupt, or cause harm to.* The lesson here with regard to the local church is that the one who corrupts or causes harm to the church will reap a similar corruption. Build on that foundation with care. Ignoring the role of the church will surely result in God's rejection of the wood, hay and stubble that represents those perhaps well-intentioned works that are performed without the blessing and oversight of the church. For the believer, removing oneself from the umbrella of the church constitutes a wound that diminishes the effectiveness of the church and places the erring believer in spiritual jeopardy.

This prominence and authority of the church is also seen in the New Testament instructions for the discipline of Christians. The Thessalonian church was cautioned to discipline some unruly members:

"⁶ Now we command you, brothers, in the name of our Lord Jesus Christ, that you keep away from any brother who is walking in idleness and not in accord with the tradition that you received from us. ⁷ For you yourselves know how you ought to imitate us, because we were not idle when we were with you, ⁸ nor did we eat anyone's bread without paying for it, but with toil and labor we worked night and day, that we might not be a burden to any of you. ⁹ It was not because we do not have that right, but to give you in ourselves an example to imitate. ¹⁰ For even when we were with you, we would give you this command: If anyone is not willing to work, let him not eat. ¹¹ For we hear that some among you walk in idleness, not busy at work, but busybodies. [12] Now such persons we command and encourage in the Lord Jesus Christ to do their work quietly and to earn their own living.

[13] As for you, brothers, do not grow weary in doing good. [14] If anyone does not obey what we say in this letter, take note of that person, and have nothing to do with him, that he may be ashamed. [15] Do not regard him as an enemy, but warn him as a brother." [84]

In today's seeker-friendly church culture it is somewhat uncommon for a church to withdraw from a brother and have no company with him. Churches are reluctant to exercise discipline, sometimes for fear of the legal implications, but as often for fear of losing the support or good will of the erring member or his family or the community. This passage makes it abundantly clear that the purpose of such discipline is to produce shame on the part of the disobedient brother that, hopefully, will lead to repentance and restoration. In this instance, the discipline was exacted because one of the members would not work; others were busybodies; some, apparently, were living disorderly lives. The church was to love them and admonish them, but if repentance was not forthcoming, they were to withdraw fellowship. The other side of the coin for church discipline is found in Hebrews 10:24-25: "And let us consider how to stir up one another to love and good works, not neglecting to meet together, as is the habit of some, but encouraging one another, and all the more as you see the Day drawing near." The assembly of believers in the church is a fellowship that provokes its members to good works. It is the opposite of the shame that they will feel should it become necessary for the church to exercise discipline by withdrawing fellowship.

The familiar passage on church discipline found in First Corinthians 5:1-5 points out the significance of the oversight of the church in a fearful way:

84　2 Thessalonians 3:6-15

"It is actually reported that there is sexual immorality among you, and of a kind that is not tolerated even among pagans, for a man has his father's wife. [2] And you are arrogant! Ought you not rather to mourn? Let him who has done this be removed from among you. [3] For though absent in body, I am present in spirit; and as if present, I have already pronounced judgment on the one who did such a thing. [4] When you are assembled in the name of the Lord Jesus and my spirit is present, with the power of our Lord Jesus, [5] you are to deliver this man to Satan for the destruction of the flesh, so that his spirit may be saved in the day of the Lord."

Is the fellowship and oversight of the local church an important consideration for the chaplain? According to scripture, exclusion from the church is comparable to delivery to "Satan for the destruction of the flesh." Certainly, the sin of the unnamed member of the church in Corinth is a most grievous one and we would not find precise equivalence with everyone who leaves the church out of his life, but it is a sin nonetheless, and a serious one at that. Apparently, a believer who is not living under the protection of the church is residing in the sphere of the devil. Not a very pleasant place to be. Why then would a minister, or any Christian, want to absent himself from the warmth and covering of the church to order their life and ministry in the world where Satan has been given some authority? One would think that a chaplain who is appointed to minister largely in a secular setting in some measure distant from the church would be especially careful to maintain an intimate relationship with his church.

The prominence of the local church in the life of every believer is shown in so many ways, that we tend to take it for granted. The Lord Jesus said He would build His church. The bulk of the New Testament was written to the churches or pastors of the churches. Epistles that were not directed to specific churches carried instructions for dissemination among the churches. Matthew 18:15-17 instructs us to bring our disputes to the church for adjudication:

> "If your brother sins against you, go and tell him his fault, between you and him alone. If he listens to you, you have gained your brother. [16] But if he does not listen, take one or two others along with you, that every charge may be established by the evidence of two or three witnesses. [17] If he refuses to listen to them, tell it to the church. And if he refuses to listen even to the church, let him be to you as a Gentile and a tax collector.

We are told here that if we neglect the counsel of the assembly we are no better off than the unsaved. Though this reference to the assembly of believers predates the establishment of the New Testament Church, it constitutes the pattern that would be embraced by the Apostles in the polity of the churches.

Another powerful illustration is seen in the ordinances of the church. The local church is the overseer of the ordinances: baptism and the Lord's Supper. Both are acts of obedience expected of all true believers. Baptism is the step of obedient testimony that pictures the believer's identification by faith with Christ in His death, burial and resurrection. The Lord Jesus Himself instructed that we should "Go ... and make disciples of all nations, *baptizing them* in the name of the Father, and of the Son, and of the Holy Spirit."[85] (Italics mine) In almost all Christian congregations, it is considered an entrance into membership in the local church.

The Lord's Supper also is a matter of obedience, and it was instituted by Christ Himself as a reminder of His death, burial and resurrection. It is intended to be a most precious

---

85   Matthew 28:20

fellowship in the church. In 1 Corinthians 11:23-34, Paul outlines instructions for the communion observance:

> For I received from the Lord what I also delivered to you, that the Lord Jesus on the night when he was betrayed took bread, [24] and when he had given thanks, he broke it, and said, "This is my body which is for you. Do this in remembrance of me." [25] In the same way also he took the cup, after supper, saying, "This cup is the new covenant in my blood. Do this, as often as you drink it, in remembrance of me." [26] For as often as you eat this bread and drink the cup, you proclaim the Lord's death until he comes.
>
> [27] Whoever, therefore, eats the bread or drinks the cup of the Lord in an unworthy manner will be guilty concerning the body and blood of the Lord. [28] Let a person examine himself, then, and so eat of the bread and drink of the cup. [29] For anyone who eats and drinks without discerning the body eats and drinks judgment on himself. [30] That is why many of you are weak and ill, and some have died. [31] But if we judged ourselves truly, we would not be judged. [32] But when we are judged by the Lord, we are disciplined so that we may not be condemned along with the world.
>
> [33] So then, my brothers, when you come together to eat, wait for one another— [34] if anyone is hungry, let him eat at home—so that when you come together it will not be for judgment. About the other things I will give directions when I come.

In verse twenty-three he states clearly that he had received the information directly from Christ. It was the command of our Lord that we do so, but we are warned that we must do so in a worthy manner. Before partaking, we are to examine ourselves so that we will not be judged. If we eat and drink unworthily we fail to discern the Lord's body. The double reference here is inescapable. A lead-in to the discussion of the Lord's Supper in the previous chapter offers insight. "I speak as to sensible people; judge for yourselves what I say. The cup of blessing that we bless, is it not a participation in the blood of Christ? The bread that we break, is it not a participation in the body of Christ? Because there is one bread, we who are many are one body, for we all partake of the one bread."[86] As partakers of Christ, we are a body of Christ. The ordinance of communion employs the bread as a type of Christ's body, but it is also true that the church is his body. The church body partakes of His body in remembrance of His death, burial and resurrection to purchase them from the marketplace of sin, until He returns to present His body spotless and holy before the Father. The biblical evidence is building and brings us to the understanding that anyone who enters chaplaincy or any other ministry in disregard of the body [the church] is in a real sense despising the body and is therefore in danger of judgment every time he participates in the communion service.

It was God's plan to establish the church so that believers would not be left to the shifting winds of error or the numbing pain of deception. Ephesians 4:8 assures us when Christ finished the work of salvation and ascended to Heaven, He "gave gifts to men" through the body [the church]:

> And he gave the apostles, the prophets, the evangelists, the shepherds and teachers, [12] to equip the saints for the work of ministry, for building up the body of Christ, [13] until we all attain to the unity of the faith and of the knowledge of the Son of God, to mature manhood, to the measure of the stature of the fullness of Christ, [14] so that we may no longer be children, tossed to and fro by the waves and carried about by every wind of doctrine, by human cunning, by craftiness in deceitful schemes. [15] Rather, speaking

---

86 1 Corinthians 10:15-17

the truth in love, we are to grow up in every way into him who is the head, into Christ, [16] from whom the whole body, joined and held together by every joint with which it is equipped, when each part is working properly, makes the body grow so that it builds itself up in love. Ephesians 4:11-16

Every need is anticipated in the gifts of God to the church. The perfection of the believers, the work of ministry, the encouragement of the Body, the unity of the faith, the knowledge of God, the fullness of our salvation, doctrinal stability, preservation of the truth, and the working out of love. There simply is no biblical pattern for ministry apart from the fellowship and oversight of the church. Furthermore, the entirety of First Corinthians chapter twelve insists that spiritual gifts given to individuals are for the edification and benefit of the body [the church] and concludes by saying, "...you are the body of Christ, and individually members of it." If one of the parts does not function, the whole body suffers.

This New Testament pattern for ministry is clearly seen in the Acts of the Apostles where we find a very distinct picture of the oversight of the church as the Gospel spread in Jerusalem, Judea, Samaria, and to the uttermost parts of the earth. Let's begin with the Church in Jerusalem.

The pattern of the New Testament church began to emerge in Acts chapter one:

Then they returned to Jerusalem from the mount called Olivet, which is near Jerusalem, a Sabbath day's journey away. [13] And when they had entered, they went up to the upper room, where they were staying, Peter and John and James and Andrew, Philip and Thomas, Bartholomew and Matthew, James the son of Alphaeus and Simon the Zealot and Judas the son of James. [14] All these with one accord were devoting themselves to prayer, together with the women and Mary the mother of Jesus, and his brothers.

[15] In those days Peter stood up among the brothers (the company of persons was in all about 120) and said, [16] "Brothers, the Scripture had to be fulfilled, which the Holy Spirit spoke beforehand by the mouth of David concerning Judas, who became a guide to those who arrested Jesus. [17] For he was numbered among us and was allotted his share in this ministry." [18] (Now this man acquired a field with the reward of his wickedness, and falling headlong he burst open in the middle and all his bowels gushed out. [19] And it became known to all the inhabitants of Jerusalem, so that the field was called in their own language Akeldama, that is, Field of Blood.) [20] "For it is written in the Book of Psalms, "May his camp become desolate, and let there be no one to dwell in it"; and "Let another take his office." Acts 1:12-20

At this first meeting, we find an assembly of 120 people who prayed together and searched the scripture. They saw in the Old Testament writings of David biblical guidance for their current situation. Peter cited Psalm 69:25[87] and Psalm 109:8[88] addressing the first order of business for those who were met in Jerusalem. There would be no need to do so unless they understood that some more formal polity was in order. The minutes of the first organizational meeting of the soon to be church in Jerusalem follows:

So one of the men who have accompanied us during all the time that the Lord Jesus went in and out among

---

87   "May their camp be a desolation; let no one dwell in their tents." Psalm 69:25

88   "May his days be few; may another take his office." Psalm 109:8

us, [22] beginning from the baptism of John until the day when he was taken up from us—one of these men must become with us a witness to his resurrection." [23] And they put forward two, Joseph called Barsabbas, who was also called Justus, and Matthias. [24] And they prayed and said, "You, Lord, who know the hearts of all, show which one of these two you have chosen [25] to take the place in this ministry and apostleship from which Judas turned aside to go to his own place." [26] And they cast lots for them, and the lot fell on Matthias, and he was numbered with the eleven apostles. Acts 1:21-26

It is significant that the Holy Spirit records that there were one hundred twenty people gathered at that time. One might expect that the eleven could have met privately to choose a successor to Judas, but in keeping with what would become the New Testament pattern for church polity, the disciples numbered were not just the Apostles and included the women. The congregation assembled on that day set aside two who met the criteria for apostleship; they prayed for guidance and direction from God; they submitted to the Providence of God in their selection; and they commissioned Matthias to his post. They did not ask for volunteers or applications, the assembly put them forth.

The church in Jerusalem experienced a rapid growth as the 120 quickly grew to thousands.

So those who received his word were baptized, and there were added that day about three thousand souls. [42] And they devoted themselves to the apostles' teaching and the fellowship, to the breaking of bread and the prayers. [43] And awe came upon every soul, and many wonders and signs were being done through the apostles. [44] And all who believed were together and had all things in common. [45] And they were selling their possessions and belongings and distributing the proceeds to all, as any had need. [46] And day by day, attending the temple together and breaking bread in their homes, they received their food with glad and generous hearts, [47] praising God and having favor with all the people. And the Lord added to their number day by day those who were being saved. Acts 2:41-47

Three thousand were added to the congregation in a great demonstration of the power of God and the working of the Holy Spirit. To be sure, there have been claims of greater response, but I know of no other occasion in History where it can be said of the multitude responding to a sermon that "they continued steadfastly in the apostles' doctrine and fellowship..." The unfortunate experience today, when we witness a great turning to Christianity, is that many, if not most, will quickly drift away when the emotion of the moment has passed. This inauguration of the church in Jerusalem was truly remarkable in that respect. Immediately, we find the believers bound together with common purpose that revolved around sound doctrine, congregational fellowship, baptism, observance of the Lord's Supper and prayer. Even in this early hour of the church, we see familiar elements of worship and polity. The Lord added to the church daily those whom He would call to salvation and they were immediately embraced into a loving fellowship where they could grow and prosper spiritually in the care of the church.

Fast forward now to Acts chapter 6 and the previously cited account[89] of the selection of servants to expand the ministry of the church, and their subsequent commissioning. The congregation acted in concert with the leadership of the apostles and the result was that "the word of God increased; and the number of the disciples multiplied in Jerusalem greatly."[90]

---

89 See previous remarks in chapter three with regard to the selection of deacons in the church in Jerusalem.

90 Acts 6:7

It is of note that the apostles communicated a clear standard for their choice, but within those parameters did not dictate the church's selection and they accepted the decision of the congregation without question or interference.

In Acts 8:1, we find another tidbit of information that will add to our understanding. It is the first New Testament reference to a church being located in a specific community, "the church in Jerusalem." Some of those who had traveled to Jerusalem for Pentecost and were saved had by now returned to their homes. Others were driven away to Judea and Samaria by the persecution that had come upon the Christians in Jerusalem. This is important, because it clearly identifies a local church and implies that there were other assemblies as well. We will find that they exercised the same authority in the lives of their members that we would correctly ascribe to the church in Jerusalem; and they cooperated together in the encouragement of the believers and in the proclamation of the faith.

[19] Now those who were scattered because of the persecution that arose over Stephen traveled as far as Phoenicia and Cyprus and Antioch, speaking the word to no one except Jews. [20] But there were some of them, men of Cyprus and Cyrene, who on coming to Antioch spoke to the Hellenists also, preaching the Lord Jesus. [21] And the hand of the Lord was with them, and a great number who believed turned to the Lord. [22] The report of this came to the ears of the church in Jerusalem, and they sent Barnabas to Antioch. [23] When he came and saw the grace of God, he was glad, and he exhorted them all to remain faithful to the Lord with steadfast purpose, [24] for he was a good man, full of the Holy Spirit and of faith. And a great many people were added to the Lord. [25] So Barnabas went to Tarsus to look for Saul, [26] and when he had found him, he brought him to Antioch.

For a whole year they met with the church and taught a great many people. And in Antioch the disciples were first called Christians.

[27] Now in these days prophets came down from Jerusalem to Antioch. [28] And one of them named Agabus stood up and foretold by the Spirit that there would be a great famine over all the world (this took place in the days of Claudius). [29] So the disciples determined, everyone according to his ability, to send relief to the brothers living in Judea. [30] And they did so, sending it to the elders by the hand of Barnabas and Saul. Acts 11:19-30

It is interesting to note that here in Acts chapter 11 we find a gathering of believers in Antioch that was comprised of many of those who had fled from Jerusalem. Some traveled to the island of Cyprus and some, apparently, dropped off in Phoenicia on the way to Antioch in Syria. As is always true of true believers, the Gospel was preached and the result was that a great number of the Greeks believed. The news of this development was taken back to the "church in Jerusalem." Note that the Christians who were in Antioch were not here referred to as a church, whereas the believers in Jerusalem were again identified as they had been in Acts 8:1 as "the church in Jerusalem." One might draw some helpful implications from these observations. Apparently, the believers in Antioch, were not yet fully organized into a local church, and the church in Jerusalem took responsibility for their welfare. Barnabas was dispatched by the church in Jerusalem to see to the care of their believers who had gone as far as Antioch. It is another implication of the oversight of the church with regard to its members. He was sent from the church in Jerusalem to mentor the new Christians in Antioch until they could establish a New Testament church and exercise biblical oversight of its members. It is at this point that the Holy Spirit refers to the Christians in Antioch as "the church." Barnabas was fulfilling the work of a church planter (missionary).[91] He found Saul and brought him to intern with the brethren in Antioch and they stayed there with them for an entire year. At this point in history, there are two recorded Christian churches, one in Jerusalem and one in Antioch.[92] It is worth noting that it was here that the term "Christian" was first employed. It was not intended as a complimentary appellation by those who coined it, but the believers gladly accepted the identification with Christ.

The next reference to the church is found in Acts 13:1-4

Now there were in the church at Antioch prophets and teachers, Barnabas, Simeon who was called Niger, Lucius of Cyrene, Manaen a member of the court of Herod the tetrarch, and Saul. ² While they were worshiping the Lord and fasting, the Holy Spirit said, "Set apart for me Barnabas and Saul for the work to which I have called them." ³ Then after fasting and praying they laid their hands on them and sent them off. ⁴ So, being sent out by the Holy Spirit, they went down to Seleucia, and from there they sailed to Cyprus.

By this time, the church in Antioch was pretty well established and it is identified as such. The "church at Antioch" was itself about to embark on the work of missions. It is pretty clear that they were concerned with God's program for the evangelization of the world. Fasting and prayer is generally associated with spiritual devotion. The Holy Spirit led them to understand that their pastor and his intern were set apart for an expanded ministry. Perhaps that is why they were fasting. Upon their recognition that Barnabas and Saul had been truly called out by God, they responded by ordaining and commissioning them.

91　The present day missionary corresponds to the evangelist noted in Eph 4:12 and elsewhere

92　No doubt there were others, but only these are recorded in the biblical record at this point.

"They laid their hands on them," and "they sent them away." It would be interesting to know if a similar action had been taken by the church in Jerusalem when Barnabas was sent to Antioch, but we are not told of the process by which the church in Jerusalem dispatched Barnabas to Antioch. It is clear that he was sent (commissioned), but the Holy Spirit has not seen fit to inform us of that matter any further. What is clear in Acts thirteen is that the laying on of the hands by the disciples in the church in Antioch in verse three is equated with being "sent out by the Holy Spirit" in verse four. The Holy Spirit moved the membership to recognize the gifts and calling of Barnabas and Saul and as a church they responded in obedience to His leading

The first missionary journey of Barnabas and Paul (no longer referenced as Saul) provides us with considerable insight on the role of the church in Christian endeavor. It was during this time that Paul began to be the more prominent preacher and Barnabas his encourager. The roles had reversed somewhat, but they comprised a missionary team. They also took along John Mark, an apprentice in ministry.[93] It was a difficult trip with opposition to the Gospel expressed in several locations. Early on in the journey John Mark left the mentorship and returned to Jerusalem,[94] a decision that would have important ramifications in the future. After traveling to many cities preaching the Gospel and encouraging those who received Christ we are told that they returned to those cities where they had been successful in gathering a group of converts. Acts 14:22, 23 tells us that they were "strengthening the souls of the disciples, encouraging them to continue in the faith, and saying that through many tribulations we must enter the kingdom of God. And when they had appointed elders for them in every church, with prayer and fasting they committed them to the Lord in whom they had believed." If we were describing their efforts today we would

---

93 Acts 13:5

94 Acts 13:13

say that they established a number of churches and appointed a pastor in each one to shepherd the believers before returning to Antioch.[95] It seems quite evident that their commission was to a church-planting ministry.

Acts 14:26-28 provides us with additional support for our understanding of the role of the church in ministry:

> ...and from there they sailed to Antioch, where they had been commended to the grace of God for the work that they had fulfilled. [27] And when they arrived and gathered the church together, they declared all that God had done with them, and how he had opened a door of faith to the Gentiles. [28] And they remained no little time with the disciples.

Two important statements in this text reinforce our understanding of the authority of the church with regard to its ministers. First, we are reminded that they were commissioned by the church in Antioch and at the end of the assignment, they returned to the commissioning church. The word *commended* employed here is from a root word [παραδίδωμι – paradidōmi] most often translated *delivered* in the sense of delivering someone over to the courts or even to death. Interestingly, the word in this form is only twice rendered commended and only when referencing the commissioning of Paul, Barnabas and Silas by the church in Antioch. These servants of God were delivered over, not to the courts for trial, but to the grace of God for testimony.

Second, when they arrived, they met with the church and reported their activities and how God had used them. It is on the basis of this that churches to this day hold their missionaries accountable for their efforts. One might tend to think that Paul, an Apostle, and certainly the most prominent person in the gathering might be excused from this accountability, but that would be a misunderstanding. The New Testament pattern is

---

95 See previous discussion of pastors in chapter one.

clear and consistent in demonstrating the accountability to the church of all its members, including those who have become prominent in ministry.

While Paul and Barnabas were resting from their difficult first missionary journey, some came from Judea promoting a doctrinal error. We read of this dispute beginning in Acts 15:1-6:

> But some men came down from Judea and were teaching the brothers, "Unless you are circumcised according to the custom of Moses, you cannot be saved." **2** And after Paul and Barnabas had no small dissension and debate with them, Paul and Barnabas and some of the others were appointed to go up to Jerusalem to the apostles and the elders about this question. **3** So, being sent on their way by the church, they passed through both Phoenicia and Samaria, describing in detail the conversion of the Gentiles, and brought great joy to all the brothers. **4** When they came to Jerusalem, they were welcomed by the church and the apostles and the elders, and they declared all that God had done with them. **5** But some believers who belonged to the party of the Pharisees rose up and said, "It is necessary to circumcise them and to order them to keep the law of Moses." **6** The apostles and the elders were gathered together to consider this matter.

This was a serious concern and scripture tells us that the church in Antioch decided to send Paul, Barnabas and some others to consult with the church and apostles in Jerusalem. It is of note that the Holy Spirit here says that they "were sent on their way *by the church*" (Italics mine) – yet another indicator of the involvement of the church in the ministry of the believer. When they got to Jerusalem, they were "welcomed by the church..." which included "the apostles and the elders." The messengers from the church in Antioch met with the pastors and apostles to consider this doctrinal matter. It cannot be overlooked that it was not the apostles alone who rendered a decision in this matter. The church was a participant in the deliberations, even though there were apostles present. Verse six verifies that "the apostles and the elders [pastors] were gathered together to consider this matter." There was input from the apostles, to be sure, namely Peter and James. They also heard testimony from the missionaries Paul and Barnabas who represented the church in Antioch. When the decision was made, Acts 15:22 records it "seemed good to the apostles and elders, *with the whole church*, to choose men from among them and send them to Antioch with Paul and Barnabas." (Italics mine) Verse twenty-three reveals that they also wrote letters that were signed by "the brothers, ... apostles and ... elders," suggesting a congregational decision. (Italics mine) Nowhere in the New Testament is there an example of the apostles making a decision regarding a member of a church without consultation with the church.

Acts 15:36-39 records a moment of sadness in the ministry of the church in Antioch:

> And after some days Paul said to Barnabas, "Let us return and visit the brothers in every city where we proclaimed the word of the Lord, and see how they are." [37] Now Barnabas wanted to take with them John called Mark. [38] But Paul thought best not to take with them one who had withdrawn from them in Pamphylia and had not gone with them to the work. [39] And there arose a sharp disagreement, so that they separated from each other. Barnabas took Mark with him and sailed away to Cyprus,

It was time for the next missionary term and as they considered their plans, the matter of whether to take John Mark with them resulted in a schism between Paul and Barnabas. Paul was adamant that John Mark had proven to be unreliable, having left them when the going got tough in Pamphylia on their first missionary journey. Barnabas was every bit as resolute that they should take him. We don't have all the details, but Acts 16:39 tells us "there arose a sharp disagreement, so that they separated from each other." Barnabas went off with John Mark to Cyprus. That's the last time we hear of Barnabas in the New Testament. John Mark was eventually restored to Paul's confidence as attested in Second Timothy 4:11 where he wrote to Timothy, "Luke alone is with me. Get Mark and bring him with you, for he is very useful to me for ministry." This is the same John Mark who Paul had refused to take on his second missionary journey. Perhaps he felt that he wasn't quite ready. We don't have that information, but we do know that eventually, John Mark was restored to usefulness in ministry.

It seems odd that there is no further biblical revelation of the ministry of Barnabas. At the outset, he was the prominent one of the missionary team sent out from the church in Antioch. There is no record that he and Paul had any other disagreement, yet Barnabas sails to Cyprus and disappears from the biblical record while Paul goes on to even more significant ministry and John Mark also is profitably used in ministry. The answer to this mystery may lie in the next verse, Acts 15:40: "Paul chose Silas and departed, *having been commended by the brothers to the grace of the Lord*. And he went through Syria and Cilicia, strengthening the churches." (Emphasis mine)   Scripture records that Paul departed "having been commended by the brothers to the grace of the Lord," which might be equated with the continued commissioning of the church. Barnabas left for Cyprus with no mention made of the blessing of the church. We have no definitive statement of scripture explaining why Barnabas disappeared from the New Testament record, but the intimation here is at least ostensible. Every other reference in the biblical record of ministerial activities recorded in the Acts of the Apostles points to the oversight of the church.

Much division in ministry is the result of a failure to submit to the authority of the church. Though some parachurch organizations are commendably structured in such a way that their ministry falls under the spiritual covering of a church, or churches cooperating in a common venture, many simply fail to understand or accept the authority of the church in the conduct of ministry. Unfortunately, there are few sermons preached and fewer books written that elucidate a New Testament pattern for the oversight of ministry. All too many sincere believers have taken it upon themselves to "sail off to Cyprus" in search of a way to serve God without the blessing or commissioning of the church. Much of the criticism for ministry that does not conform to the New Testament pattern must be placed squarely on churches that have abrogated their responsibility to oversee and discipline its members. No doubt, much of the parachurch movement has emerged, because they have grown impatient with either the lethargy or the worldliness of their church. It's easy to understand their zeal, but it does not excuse the disobedience of ministry lacking the sanctifying oversight of the church. Sadly, in the end it will be found to be wood, hay and stubble.

On May 12, 1962, General Douglas MacArthur delivered his farewell speech to the Corps of Cadets at West Point. It was a crowning moment in the life of both the general and the cadets. General MacArthur was a West Point graduate who devoted his life to the service of his country. His accomplishments in war and in peace were astounding, perhaps more notable than any general in our nation's history. I am struck by his remarks on that occasion.

> "In my dreams I hear again the crash of guns, the rattle of musketry, the strange, mournful mutter of the battlefield. But in the evening of my memory I come back to West Point. Always there echoes and re-echoes: Duty, Honor, Country.

Today marks my final roll call with you. But I want you to know that when I cross the river, my last conscious thoughts will be of the Corps, and the Corps, and the Corps"

We are in a struggle for the souls of men. The battle rages about us. On every side are distractions, destruction, disaster and defeat, but Christ Jesus the Lord has promised "I will build my church; and the gates of Hell shall not prevail against it." For over two thousand years, the Captain of our souls has guided His ministers and His flock to battle under the banner of the church. If we are to remain faithful to our Savior, we must honor and edify His church, for it is the only institution on earth that He has appointed for the growth and discipline of the believer and the proclamation of the Gospel.

The church is the nursery where the struggling babe in Christ begins to grasp the blessings of God; it is the teacher that opens the Word of God; the finishing school that brings believers to maturity; the administrator of the ordinances; the arbiter of disputes; the soother of hurts; the voice of warning; the comfort in sorrow; the encouragement in trial; the help in time of need; the caretaker of the widow and the fatherless; the administrator of discipline; the bishop of ministry; the defender of the faith; the herald of the good news; the salt and light of the culture; the referee of orthodoxy and the conduit of commission.

As we consider the pressing needs and opportunities of chaplaincy, let us submit to God's plan and let us bring our ambition, aspiration and abundance to the oversight of the church and the church and the church in obedience to the Head of the church, the Lord Jesus Christ.

~ CHAPTER FIVE ~

THE CHAPLAIN AND PLURALISM

plu·ral·ism
Pronunciation: `'plur-a-"li-zam`
Function: *noun*
1 : the holding of two or more offices or positions
(as benefices) at the same time
2 : the quality or state of being plural
3 a : a theory that there are more than one or more
than two kinds of ultimate reality **b** : a theory that
reality is composed of a plurality of entities
4 a : a state of society in which members of diverse
ethnic, racial, religious, or social groups maintain
an autonomous participation in and development
of their traditional culture or special interest within
the confines of a common civilization **b** : a concept,
doctrine, or policy advocating this state[96]

Every chaplain has been confronted with pluralism;
sometimes as an encouragement; sometimes as a warning;
and sometimes as a weapon. As our culture has become more
secular, pluralism has been viewed by some as a threat; by some
as a defense against the influence of Christianity; by some as a
protection against the persuasion of any divergent viewpoint; and
by some as a natural and desirable outcome in an increasingly
diverse culture. At some point, depending upon the person's
understanding of pluralism, all of these impressions can be seen

as accurate. The pressing question that must be answered is whether pluralism prevents a bible-believing Christian minister from performing the duties of a chaplain without compromising his doctrinal beliefs. The deterrents most often cited are what I call the three P's — *pluralism, prayer* and *proselytism,* which we will consider in order in this and the following two chapters.

There is little doubt that the perception of pluralism has unnecessarily driven many ministers from the consideration of chaplaincy. On occasion, it has been an excuse for otherwise competent chaplains to shirk their responsibility as a witness for Christ. That, too, is gratuitous. Some have hidden behind pluralism to avoid confrontation that may be entirely necessary. One thing is certain. Christian chaplains must understand pluralism and learn to minister in a pluralistic culture if they are to conduct an effective ministry. It begins with the realization that pluralism need not be a hindrance if properly understood.

In some respects, times have not changed all that much since the founding of the church. Our Lord Jesus and the early disciples faced many of the same challenges; endured many of the same criticisms; and agonized over much the same opposition. The Jews during the ministry of the First Century church lived in a culture dominated by a Roman government that promoted the worship of many gods. They were tolerated by the Romans largely for political reasons. Concessions were made toward their religious concerns as a matter of convenience, not necessarily as a matter of conviction. There were economic considerations effecting the acceptance or rejection of both the Jewish and emerging Christian faith groups as witnessed by the near riot recorded in Acts chapter 19 over the effect on the manufacture of idols caused by the success of Christian preaching.

Today, we live and minister in a culture that brings together divergent ethnicities, religions, governments, and special interests. The world is shrinking. Just thirty or forty years ago we sent missionaries off on a boat to far away places where we would not have contact for months. Often it took weeks to receive a written report. Today, we tap out instant messages to the same locations on a daily basis, providing us with a much broader understanding of other cultures and the challenges confronting missionaries. There is hardly a corner of the earth where we will not have access to a visual news report when a significant event takes place. During hurricane Katrina in 2005, we viewed the crisis in progress, sometimes learning of the situation before the authorities were sent to provide relief. This accessibility to events was repeated in 2010 when the Deep Water Horizon oil platform exploded resulting in months of mitigation. We are engaged in a war against terrorism brought about by religious intolerance complicated by schisms among those who can agree on nothing except that they hate Israel. The centuries long enmity between Arab and Jew threatens world peace. The Al Aqsa Martyrs Brigade, al-Qa'ida, HAMAS, and the IRA are just four of hundreds of known organizations that at one time or another have taken their religious bigotry to the level of murder. Is it any wonder that the idea of pluralism is confusing to many?

Pluralism is like ice cream. It comes in flavors. The question "What is pluralism?" asked of a large group of chaplains received almost as many different answers as there were people. To one it meant respect; to another acceptance; to another restriction; yet another thought of it as opposition. Each had a different concept and all agreed that it was a somewhat ambiguous concept. Most were suspicious of pluralism's intention and all agreed that it was a fact of life. It is interesting to note that so many people have such strong opinions with such disparate understanding of what it is. The dictionary definition with which we opened this chapter merely points to the obvious state of our culture, a smorgasbord of diverse palates, but many in the religious realm bring their own tastes and recipes to the table. Therein lies the problem that must be faced in any endeavor to provide effective chaplain ministry.

D.A. Carson, Research Professor of New Testament at Trinity Evangelical Divinity School suggests that there are three distinct views of pluralism. The first of these he calls *empirical pluralism,* which he defines as "the growing diversity in our culture."[97] It is simply the recognition that pluralism happens, and it has occurred in the United States in abundance.

> "Consider, for example, the remarkable ethnic diversity in America. The United States is the largest Jewish, Irish, and Swedish nation in the world; it is the second largest black nation, and soon it will become the third largest Hispanic nation. Moreover, these large proportions reveal nothing about the enormous diversity generated by countless smaller ethnic and racial communities. Compiling equally remarkable statistics in almost every other plane of American culture is an easy matter."[98]

These ethnic balances also have an effect on the religious makeup of our communities and pose some interesting challenges. For instance, the rapid growth in Hispanic population has brought a significant increase in the Roman Catholic population at a time when the number of Catholic priests is declining, which tends to result in an increased utilization of priests from other cultures. The growing influence of millions of illegal immigrants has a significant political impact as witnessed by large scale demonstrations throughout the United States. In addition, there are an increasing number of smaller, but growing religious sects adding to the mix. Carson goes on to say:

> "There are substantial numbers of Hindus and Buddhists who have emigrated to the West, and who are now slowly winning converts. The familiar cults

97 D. A. Carson, The Gagging of God, Christianity Confronts Pluralism, (Grand Rapids, MI, Zondervan, 1996), p 13.
98 Ibid., 14

are holding their own; some of them, like the Mormons, are growing fairly rapidly. Numerous studies document the Rise of New Age religions and the revitalization of various forms of neo-paganism. Not long ago witches' covens were virtually unknown; now they advertise in the newspapers. Current immigration patterns are bringing in more and more people with little heritage in the Judeo-Christian tradition, and this fact doubles the impact of the number of people within the country who for various reasons have lost or abandoned the tradition. None of this was foreseen by the founding Fathers; little of it was foreseen forty years ago."[99]

One can not deny the existence of these trends in our society. The demographic is changing and it is incumbent on Christian ministers to strategize an effective means of ministry for the reality of what Carson terms empirical pluralism. This is especially true of chaplaincy, since chaplains in particular minister in the general society outside the church fellowship. Christian chaplains have an opportunity to share the claims of Christ in an ever widening cultural venue and it should be taken as a welcome challenge to look beyond our doorstep to the uttermost parts of the earth without ever having to leave home

A second definition of pluralism is what Carson terms *cherished pluralism*. The belief that the diversity and variety in our culture is a good thing and it is to be desired. Empirical pluralism says that we live in a society which is plural in the sense that there are a variety of cultures, religions and lifestyles. Cherished pluralism moves beyond this realization and affirms the integrity of that diversity. "In other words, the reality, empirical pluralism, has become a value in itself, even a priority: it is cherished."[100] Historically, we in the United States have taken a significant amount of pride in our heritage as a

99 Ibid., 15
100 Ibid., 18

"melting pot." This view of pluralism is; therefore, nothing new to our experience. Where else in the world have so many come together in harmony to accomplish so much in the pursuit of freedom? Our motto is *E pluribus unum*, meaning out of many, one. No doubt our founding Fathers made reference to the union of the thirteen colonies, but the slogan became prophetic in its application. There is nothing particularly new about cherished pluralism.

A third understanding; however, has proven to be problematic. Carson refers to it as *philosophical pluralism* (or hermeneutical pluralism). Philosophical pluralism holds that there can be no opinion or religion that claims to possess the absolute truth. Carson puts it this way:

> "This is, by far, the most serious development. Philosophical pluralism has generated many approaches in support of one stance: namely, that any notion that a particular ideological or religious claim is intrinsically superior to another is *necessarily* wrong. The only absolute creed is the creed of pluralism. No religion has the right to pronounce itself right or true, and the others false, or even (in the majority view) relatively inferior."[101]

This is the expression of pluralism that most offends, and in fact *must* offend, the Christian chaplain. The very foundation of the Christian faith is the understanding that the death, burial and resurrection of the Lord Jesus Christ as a propitiatory sacrifice for sin is the only means of salvation, and apart from faith in Him, there is no justification before God. The implementation of philosophical (or hermeneutical) pluralism is nothing less than a gauntlet of challenge to everything that is held precious by Christians. It is tolerance run amuck; thinking that escapes all reason. To fully embrace this view, a true Christian would

---

101 Ibid., 19

have to abandon his faith and renounce his Lord. Matthew 10:32-33 comes to mind: "So everyone who acknowledges me before men, I also will acknowledge before my Father who is in heaven, but whoever denies me before men, I also will deny before my Father who is in heaven."

Philosophical pluralism challenges Christianity in a different way than that which the American church has confronted heretofore. As the Twentieth Century emerged, biblical Christians in the United States faced the intrusion of a religious modernism articulated progressively as Liberalism, Neo-liberalism, and Neo-orthodoxy. These ecumenical expressions trended in the direction of syncretism, that is, a blend of different systems of philosophical or religious beliefs and practices into a single one-world church. Such was the cherished dream of the World Council of Churches and its American counterpart, the National Council of Churches. Syncretism sought to find spiritual truth in the amalgamation of religions. This approach is rightfully rejected by those who insist upon the Bible as the only rule of Christian faith and practice. It is important to understand that pluralism is not syncretism. In fact, philosophical pluralism precludes the thinking of syncretists by denying that there can be any objective truth. The only absolute, according to this radical form of pluralism, is that there is no absolute; the only doctrinal error is that there can be doctrinal error; the only immorality is that one can be held out as immoral. The one unexplainable exception to that, of course, is that pluralism is seen to be the truth. It's an ideal philosophy for those who believe nothing and insist that others share their ignorance.

There should be little concern with regard to what Carson terms empirical pluralism. It is nothing more than a recognition and acceptance of diversity in our culture. It is in the nature of Christian witness to extend love to all men, regardless of ethnic origin or religious preference. Leviticus 19:33-34 makes it clear that there is a biblical expectation of such: "When a stranger sojourns with you in your land, you shall not do him wrong. You shall treat the stranger who sojourns with you as the native among you, and you shall love him as yourself for you were strangers in the land of Egypt: I am the LORD your God." This Old Testament admonition is consistent with the New Testament insistence of Romans 12:18: "If possible, so far as it depends on you, live peaceably with all." Even beyond that, Galatians 6:10 insists: "So then, as we have opportunity, let us do good to everyone, and especially to those who are of the household of faith." How foolish it would be to send missionaries to the far corners of the earth to evangelize the world and then turn away from those who would come to our shores. The debate, then, hinges on the distinctive of what Carson terms *cherished pluralism* and *philosophical pluralism*, and whether either or both pose a threat to the conscience or performance of Christian chaplains. Though clearly Carson has put forth the more comprehensive and scholarly treatment, for simplicity, I would combine his concepts of empirical and cherished pluralism in the single category of *common pluralism*, and treat the philosophical iteration as *radical pluralism*.

Common pluralism is indeed the darling of our culture, especially in the educational, media and religious communities. Laws have been passed mandating diversity in every aspect of our society, and we have grown accustomed to it. The concern for chaplaincy is whether this understanding of plurality and its demand for tolerance offers a venue for ministry or presents a barrier to ministry. In truth, there have been many war stories telling of the opposition to Christian expression resultant from the advocacy of radical pluralism that would not be true in the culture of common pluralism. There is a tolerance that is entirely consistent with a biblical expression of ministry. It would be unwise to "throw out the baby with the bathwater" when we consider the demands of ministry in a pluralistic environment. Common pluralism does not mandate the abandonment of Christian convictions, nor does it prohibit its expression. It does require that we give thoughtful consideration to the attitude and demeanor of Christian outreach. It is important that chaplains and chaplaincies understand that the constitutional requirement for government agencies to grant equal validity to all religious views does not mean that Christian ministers must personally accept those views. A chaplain does not have to become a pluralist to minister in a pluralistic setting. One would also presume that even the government is not expected to permit a religious expression that threatens the safety or freedoms of its citizens. Free exercise of religion, for instance, requires that government not interfere with the operation of a mosque, but may take steps to arrest those within the mosque that plan terrorist attacks or promote some other unlawful activity.

This understanding of pluralism has become a cherished institution honored by the majority in just about every segment of our culture. It seems to work pretty well with possibly the exception of the political arena where legislators regularly mistreat each other with intolerance that would be discouraged by their own laws if entered into by the people. Common pluralism does not mandate that Christians agree with the doctrinal views or lifestyles of unbelievers, but it calls for a respectful tolerance from all religious communities and an expectation that they will honor each other's human rights. This is not inconsistent with biblical principles such as that previously mentioned: "If possible, so far as it depends on you, live peaceably with all." [102]

What Carson calls philosophical pluralism, which I have termed *radical pluralism*, takes the concept of tolerance to a ridiculous level. It has changed the very meaning of tolerance, which, in the final analysis, excludes the rights of Christians and others who hold to an understanding that there is an objective truth that labels opposing views as errant. John Piper warns of the transition from true biblical tolerance to this extreme understanding of tolerance if we embrace this form of pluralism:

---

102 Rom 12:18

"Beware of replacing real truth-based tolerance with spurious professional tolerance. Once upon a time tolerance was the power that kept lovers of competing faiths from killing each other. It was the principle that put freedom above forced conversion. It was rooted in the truth that coerced conviction is no conviction. That is true tolerance. But now the new professional tolerance denies that there *are* any competing faiths; they only complement each other. It denounces not only the effort to *force* conversions but also the idea that any conversion may be necessary. It holds the conviction that no religious conviction should claim superiority over another. In this way, peaceful parity among professionals can remain intact, and none need be persecuted for the stumbling block of the cross (Gal 5:11)."[103]

So then, when a chaplain is told that he must minister in a pluralistic culture, what does that mean? Is he to simply understand and respect the diversity of the community and extend kindness without prejudice? Is he to take a further step to facilitate the differing religious needs of those to whom he ministers? Is he free to hold his beliefs openly? May he share his belief with others in a respectful way? Must he embrace the validity of aberrant views and lifestyles? The answers to those questions depend largely on how you define pluralism; how these differing definitions relate to the specific warrants or restrictions that may be placed on a chaplain. Chaplains, on the other hand, must consider whether the restrictions placed on their ministry are such that they can no longer participate in good conscience. That dilemma is more or less problematic depending upon the particular chaplaincy. Not all chaplaincies present the same challenges. Unfortunately, concern about pluralism has led some fundamental and evangelical ministers

---

103   John Piper, Brothers We Are Not Professionals, xi

to unnecessarily conclude they may not in good conscience engage in chaplaincy in a pluralistic setting.

In the military, there are relatively clear guidelines that focus on the preservation of religious freedom for all servicemen and servicewomen. Military chaplains are seen as the guarantors of the free exercise of religion for everyone assigned to their pastoral care. Military chaplains are responsible to their endorsers for their religious views and duties and; therefore, cannot be required to participate in any rite or function that is contrary to their religious beliefs. In that sense, chaplains have the right to the free exercise of their own religion, and in exchange, they must be willing to provide the same opportunity to those who espouse a different religious understanding or, for that matter, a preference for no religion at all. It is the basis on which chaplains are permitted to serve in the armed forces as military officers paid by the United States government. Some may have heartburn over the requirement that a military chaplain must make provision for the religious needs of non-Christians, but it is no more than the expectation that a Christian would have of a chaplain of another faith or tradition. The expectation is not that the chaplain must adopt or even accept the views of other religions, but that he is willing to provide a caring ministry to those of other faiths if called upon to do so. When the requested ministry crosses the threshold of the chaplains doctrinal comfort he is expected to make other provision for the needs to be met if necessary. Often, it is simply a matter of a phone call to obtain the involvement of someone who understands the religious needs of the serviceperson who desires assistance. We see then that the ministry of military chaplaincy is clearly within the understanding of common pluralism.

Police chaplains operate in very much the same way. They are made available to assist to those who comprise the law enforcement community, and often to citizens who are in crisis as the result of some traumatic occurrence. The police chaplain has access to a culture that is mostly closed to the average person and; therefore, is given a remarkable opportunity for witness. Like the military chaplain, they must be able to minister to all faiths and persuasions in a compassionate manner. It is sometimes necessary to set aside their personal disgust of the views and lifestyle of a victim in the hope that compassion shown in the time of crisis will result in an opportunity to provide spiritual guidance, or referral to such, in due time. The same would be expected of a pastor who was called upon to encourage someone in trauma. The onset of a crisis is typically not the most opportune time to obtain spiritual decisions, since the victim is probably suffering from cortical inhibition and is hardly in a position to make important commitments. Fire department chaplains have a ministry similar to that of the police chaplain and most of the same considerations apply. They both typically minister in an environment of common pluralism.

Prison and jail chaplains have a somewhat different challenge. Much of their efforts are directed toward providing religious services and personal counseling for inmates. In some instances, they may also provide ministerial assistance to the correctional officers. As a general rule; however, it is difficult to minister to both prisoners and law enforcement simultaneously. The realities of a pluralistic culture will often require that they make access available to ministers of other faiths as well. Generally speaking, jail and prison chaplains also function in the arena of common pluralism, though there have been disturbing reports of legal decisions by activist judges that threaten to severely limit the value of prison chaplaincy. One example is a chaplain who was disciplined by the court for his unwillingness to accept a homosexual inmate as director of a Christian choir. This was an encroachment into radical pluralism that extends beyond the reasonable expectations of tolerance and which resulted in government interference with the free exercise of religion. Oddly enough, it has sometimes been the homosexual agenda, not the ecumenical or pluralist agenda that has been the instrument of an erosion of religious freedom in the United

States.[104] The homosexual community typically embraces a more radical view of pluralism, because they rightly see the proclamation of the Word of God as a threat to the acceptance of their lifestyle and fear the application of scripture. One might accurately appropriate the term *bibleophobia.*

Probably the most restrictive chaplaincy and that which may function closer to the borders of radical pluralism is found in healthcare. The requirements mandated by some clinical pastoral education programs are very restrictive of religious expression. Some hospital chaplaincies, for example, have turned away ministers who will not endorse the homosexual agenda, and strict oversight of chaplain ministry to prevent even the hint of proselytizing is common. In some instances, Christian organizations like the Healthcare Chaplains Ministry Association (HCMA) are able to recruit, train and provide chaplains who are not on the hospital payroll, thereby avoiding some of the more restrictive aspects imposed by secular oversight. The Veterans Administration conducts an extensive chaplaincy program in VA hospitals and clinics that functions on much the same basis as the military. Healthcare chaplains are able to bring words of comfort and faith to those who may be facing spiritual concerns at a time when they are confronted by serious, perhaps even life threatening illness or injury. It is a valuable ministry that must be conducted with sensitivity and care.

The Health Insurance Portability and Accountability Act (HIPAA) which restricts disclosure of health information that identifies patients has, in some instances, made pastoral visitation in hospitals more difficult. Some hospitals are reluctant to allow a pastor access to patients unless there is a specific request by the patient. In some healthcare facilities, the patient will be asked upon admission if they desire spiritual care and if they decline, no minister will be allowed access unless the patient explicitly asks for him by name. In some instances, this misapplication

---

104   At the writing of this book, it is too soon to forecast the impact of a revocation of the "Don't Ask, Don't Tell" policy in the Armed Forces. It could prove to be the next and most serious challenge to the conduct of Christian chaplaincy.

of the provisions of the law has been employed to restrict the activities of even hospital chaplains. There has been considerable confusion and discussion in healthcare chaplaincies about these provisions and in particular the matter of distinguishing between healthcare chaplains and community clergy. Trained hospital chaplains are sometimes considered a part of the health care team and as such given access to patient information that is denied to general clergy. Strict application of HIPAA as defined by some law firms has challenged that practice.

Many chaplains function in corporations, sports organizations, service clubs and recreational activities not associated with governmental or civic entities. In these instances religious parameters will be established by the individual company or organization. There has been a concerted effort on the part of organizations such as the American Civil Liberties Union, People For The American Way, Freedom From Religion Foundation and others of that ilk to restrict access to religious expression in this venue as they have in the public arena. Too often even private companies are reluctant to face the threat of the radical pluralists, fearing intimidation and expensive legal costs.

Pluralism is! It is a fact of life in our modern culture. Christian chaplains must learn to deal with it and when appropriate even embrace it. Christian ministry has nothing to fear from common pluralism and, fortunately, most chaplaincies are not required to function in an arena of radical pluralism. The New Testament pattern of ministry provides us with ample evidence of effective ministry despite the challenges of the world order. There is a biblical strategy for ministry in a pluralistic culture.

Be gracious. Acts chapter 19 offers an example of such ministry in a pagan setting:

> For a man named Demetrius, a silversmith, who
> made silver shrines of Artemis, brought no little

business to the craftsmen. [25] These he gathered together, with the workmen in similar trades, and said, "Men, you know that from this business we have our wealth. [26] And you see and hear that not only in Ephesus but in almost all of Asia this Paul has persuaded and turned away a great many people, saying that gods made with hands are not gods. [27] And there is danger not only that this trade of ours may come into disrepute but also that the temple of the great goddess Artemis may be counted as nothing, and that she may even be deposed from her magnificence, she whom all Asia and the world worship."

[28] When they heard this they were enraged and were crying out, "Great is Artemis of the Ephesians!" [29] So the city was filled with the confusion, and they rushed together into the theater, dragging with them Gaius and Aristarchus, Macedonians who were Paul's companions in travel. [30] But when Paul wished to go in among the crowd, the disciples would not let him. [31] And even some of the Asiarchs, who were friends of his, sent to him and were urging him not to venture into the theater. [32] Now some cried out one thing, some another, for the assembly was in confusion, and most of them did not know why they had come together. [33] Some of the crowd prompted Alexander, whom the Jews had put forward. And Alexander, motioning with his hand, wanted to make a defense to the crowd. [34] But when they recognized that he was a Jew, for about two hours they all cried out with one voice, "Great is Artemis of the Ephesians!"

[35] And when the town clerk had quieted the crowd, he said, "Men of Ephesus, who is there who does not know that the city of the Ephesians is temple keeper of the great Artemis, and of the sacred stone that fell from the sky? [36] Seeing then that these things cannot

> be denied, you ought to be quiet and do nothing rash. [37]
> For you have brought these men here who are neither
> sacrilegious nor blasphemers of our goddess. [38] If
> therefore Demetrius and the craftsmen with him have
> a complaint against anyone, the courts are open, and
> there are proconsuls. Let them bring charges against
> one another. [39] But if you seek anything further, it shall
> be settled in the regular assembly. [40] For we really
> are in danger of being charged with rioting today,
> since there is no cause that we can give to justify this
> commotion." [41] And when he had said these things, he
> dismissed the assembly. Acts 19:24-41

In Acts chapter 19 we see demonstrated both the positive effect
of Christian ministry and the opposition that often follows it.
In this instance, there was a commercial interest involving the
manufacture of idols that was impacted by the success of the
ministry of the church in Ephesus. Paul was there with some
companions and a great number had believed. There can be no
question that the Word of God had been faithfully preached, for
verse 20 tells us "So the word of the Lord continued to increase
and prevail mightily." Paul would say of his ministry in Ephesus
"I did not shrink from declaring to you the whole counsel of
God."[105] The opposition, namely Demetrius and his cohorts in
the trade union, had two concerns. One was economic. They
were troubled that the influence of Christianity had resulted or
would result in the declination of the sale of idols. The artisans
in this account appear similar to modern day trade unions
and they responded in much the same manner. The other was
spiritual. They anticipated that as a result of Christian teaching,
many would despise the temple of their goddess Artemis
(known also as Diana) and that she would fall into disrepute.
They stirred up a near riot to petition the authorities to put a stop
to the preaching of the Gospel. This was a direct assault on the

---

105 Acts 20:27

Christian faith, not unlike some sects today that would simply prohibit any disparate belief. The Christians were not pluralists by any means, but this event demonstrates how Christians may have a meaningful ministry in the face of fierce opposition. The detractors were unsuccessful in their efforts. The Christians in Ephesus had faithfully proclaimed doctrinal truth, but did so with a kind spirit and respectful demeanor. We gather this from the testimony of the town clerk who calmed the crowd by pointing out that no valid charges could be brought against the Christians because they were "neither sacrilegious nor blasphemers of [their] goddess." Certainly, the believers spoke boldly of the one true God and they turned many away from the worship of idols but, apparently, they did so with a civility that spoke louder than the shouting mob. Their approach was not to *force* a conversion upon them with violence or legislation, but to demonstrate the grace of Christ as they proclaimed the truth.

Lest anyone think that these believers somehow compromised the Gospel, we must point out that when Paul, who was in Ephesus with them during these events, returned to Ephesus and called together the elders of the church, he testified that he "did not shrink from declaring to [them] anything that was profitable, and teaching [them] in public and from house to house, testifying both to Jews and to Greeks of repentance toward God and of faith in our Lord Jesus Christ."[106] This event may be taken as an encouragement to faithfully persist in ministry, even in the face of the demands of pluralism, whether common or radical. To be sure, there comes a time for battle, but we must bear in mind that it is God's battle, not ours. Our requirement is to remain faithful to our calling.

Be a servant. Another valuable principle in ministry in a pluralistic culture is to show a sensitivity to the cultural context when it can be done without misrepresentation or compromise of biblical principles. The best way to demonstrate that is to become a servant.

---

106 Acts 20:20, 21

Have this mind among yourselves, which is yours in Christ Jesus, [6] who, though he was in the form of God, did not count equality with God a thing to be grasped, [7] but made himself nothing, taking the form of a servant, being born in the likeness of men. [8] And being found in human form, he humbled himself by becoming obedient to the point of death, even death on a cross. Philippians 2:5-8

Paul demonstrated this attitude of sensitive servanthood in 1 Corinthians 9:19-23

For though I am free from all, I have made myself a servant to all, that I might win more of them. [20] To the Jews I became as a Jew, in order to win Jews. To those under the law I became as one under the law (though not being myself under the law) that I might win those under the law. [21] To those outside the law I became as one outside the law (not being outside the law of God but under the law of Christ) that I might win those outside the law. [22] To the weak I became weak, that I might win the weak. I have become all things to all people, that by all means I might save some. [23] I do it all for the sake of the gospel, that I may share with them in its blessings.

In citing this passage, I do not intend a common understanding and practice of simply incorporating the mores and methods of the world order into ministry. That is not the meaning of this text. Paul said in Second Corinthians 5:20, "we are ambassadors for Christ, God making his appeal through us. We implore you on behalf of Christ, be reconciled to God." Men ought always to be reconciled to God. It is not the other way around. What is too common today, I fear, is the attempt to reconcile God to men. Sadly, ministry that focuses more on the creature than on the

Creator[107] simply incorporates the affectations of the world in an attempt to make Christianity more attractive to the flesh. That is not what Paul intended in the passage cited. Paul's declaration that he had "become all things to all people, that by all means [he] might save some," must be understood in the context of his previous assertion, "though I am free from all I have made myself a servant to all that I might win more of them." These two statements are connected. Paul was not suggesting that he embraced the base and vile things of the culture to gain their acceptance, but that he submitted himself to the same limitations so that he might demonstrate his commitment to the Gospel. The gifted commentator Matthew Henry put it this way:

> "He did not despise nor judge them, but became as one of them, forbore to use his liberty for their sake, and was careful to lay no stumbling-block in their way. Where any, through the weakness of their understanding, or the strength of their prejudices, were likely to fall into sin, or fall off from the gospel into heathen idolatry, through his use of his liberty, he refrained himself. He denied himself for their sakes, that he might insinuate into their affections, and gain their souls. In short, *he became all things to all men, that he might by all means* (all lawful means) *gain some.* He would not sin against God to save the soul of his neighbour, but he would very cheerfully and readily deny himself. The rights of God he could not give up, but he might resign his own, and he very often did so for the good of others."[108]

The deeper meaning of First Corinthians 9:20-23 is the gain found by foregoing ones own liberties so as not to place a

---

107   Romans 1:25
108   Henry, Matthew. (1996, c1991). *Matthew Henry's commentary on the whole Bible : Complete and unabridged in one volume* (1 Co 9:19). Peabody: Hendrickson.

stumbling block in the path of others. To apply any other meaning to Paul's statement would constitute a contradiction of his negation of sin in Romans 6:1, 2 saying, "What shall we say then? Are we to continue in sin, that grace may abound? By no means! How can we who died to sin, still live in it?" The Pulpit Commentary presents a similar explanation:

> "It should be carefully observed that St. Paul is here describing the innocent concessions and compliances which arise from the harmless and generous condescension of a loving spirit. He never sank into the fear of man, which made Peter at Antioch unfaithful to his real principles. He did not allow men to form from his conduct any mistaken inference as to his essential views. He waived his personal predilections in matters of indifference which only affected "the infinitely little...."[109]

> "...In other words, I so far became to the heathen as a heathen (Rom 2:12), that I never willfully insulted their beliefs (Acts 19:37) nor shocked their prejudices, but on the contrary, judged them with perfect forbearance (Acts 17:30) and treated them with invariable courtesy. St. Paul tried to look at every subject, so far as he could do so innocently, from their point of view (Acts 17) He defended their gospel liberty, and had intercourse with Gentile converts on terms of perfect equality (Gal 2:12)."[110]

The deeper understanding of First Corinthians 9:19-23 points us to the example of a sensitive servant of God who denied his own freedoms in the pursuit of the salvation of others. It is nothing less than what is expected of a servant-chaplain who is granted the

---

109   *The Pulpit Commentary: 1 Corinthians.* 2004 (H. D. M. Spence-Jones, Ed.) (289). Bellingham, WA: Logos Research Systems, Inc.
110   *Ibid.*

opportunity to minister with compassion in a multi-cultural and/ or multi-denominational setting. When the ministry of chaplaincy becomes an issue of the chaplain's rights, ministry is distorted and rendered ineffective. It isn't about the chaplain, it's about those to whom the chaplain ministers. Paul and the early church understood that.

Be godly. A third effective tool of chaplain ministry in a pluralistic setting is a godly example. There is always a temptation in chaplaincy to be one of the boys and there are many opportunities to succumb to such enticement. As cited earlier, the nature of chaplain ministry demands a mature understanding of the faith and a proven commitment to godliness. In the midst of chaos, the chaplain is the one person who must remain confident. When profanity and foolish talking prevails, the chaplain must have a sanctified tongue. When sin abounds, the chaplain must demonstrate the righteousness of God. Such a testimony will cut through the fog of indifference and even opposition; and preach a sermon that cannot be ignored. Alas, often it is otherwise when the chaplain joins in course talk and profanity; when the chaplain amuses himself with the gutter joke; or when the chaplain can speak only of worldly diversion. One of the most attractive tools for ministry in a pluralistic culture is a working example of godliness. No regulation or expectation can prohibit that.

The message of the apostles is summarized in Acts 4:12: "And there is salvation in no one else, for there is no other name under heaven given among men by which we must be saved." That Name, of course, is Christ Jesus, the Lord. Every committed Christian chaplain desires to communicate that essential message. It is the very thing that radical pluralists wish to eliminate. The key to the opportunity is found in the very next verse, Acts 4:13: "Now when they saw the boldness of Peter and John, and perceived that they were uneducated, common men, they were astonished. And they recognized that they had been with Jesus." It is not the pedigree of the chaplain that opens the door to Christian witness. It is the identification with Christ. The necessary education and experience will equip the chaplain to address the theological and practical concerns of ministry, but it is his godliness that will win him the right to speak. We ought to think of chaplaincy as the ministry of presence, because it points to the presence of God, not the presence of the chaplain. There is no better way to demonstrate that than to model a godly life; a life that models the truth of Galatians 5:22, 23, "But the fruit of the Spirit is love, joy, peace, patience, kindness, goodness, faithfulness, gentleness, self-control; against such things there is no law." No amount of pluralist rhetoric or opposition can restrict the outworking of the Spirit of God seen in the life of a truly committed Christian chaplain. It is a difficult, but necessary objective to be sure. "Indeed, all who desire to live a godly life in Christ Jesus will be persecuted,"[111] but the other side of that coin is that "the prayer of a righteous person has great power as it is working."[112]

The most powerful answer to the demands of pluralism in chaplaincy is not isolation or political action or vitriol or denial. Rather, it is a gracious ministry offered by a servant-chaplain who is committed to godly living that models the heart of Christ. Be gracious; be a servant; and be godly. Christian chaplains need not fear the threat of even radical pluralism and quit the field as is too often the case. We must continue to be alert to opportunities for ministry. There may come a day when the door is closed, but that day is not yet upon us. Christian chaplains have nothing to fear from pluralism, for we have the assurance of scripture that "…you are from God and have overcome them, for he who is in you is greater than he who is in the world."[113]

---

111   2 Timothy 3:12
112   James 5:16
113   1 John 4:4

CHAPTER SIX

THE CHAPLAIN AND PRAYER

O LORD
In prayer I launch far out into the eternal world,
      and on that broad ocean my soul triumphs
      over all evils on the shores of mortality.
Time, with its gay amusements and cruel disappointments
      never appears so inconsiderate as then.
In prayer I see myself as nothing;
      I find my heart going after thee with intensity,
      and long with vehement thirst to live to thee.
Blessed be the strong gales of the Spirit
      that speed me on my way to the New Jerusalem.
In prayer all things here below vanish,
      and nothing seems important
      but holiness of heart and the salvation of others.
In prayer all my worldly cares, fears, anxieties disappear,
      and are of as little significance as a puff of wind.
In prayer my soul inwardly exults with lively thoughts
      at what thou art doing for thy church,
      and I long that thou shouldest get thyself a great
      name from sinners returning to Zion.
In prayer I am lifted above the frowns and flatteries of
      life,
      and taste heavenly joys;
      entering into the eternal world
      I can give myself to thee with all my heart,
      to be thine for ever.

> In prayer I can place all my concerns in thy hands,
> > to be entirely at thy disposal,
> > having no will or interest of my own.
> In prayer I can intercede for my friends, ministers,
> > sinners, the church, thy kingdom to come,
> > with greatest freedom, ardent hopes,
> > as a son to his father,
> > as a lover to the beloved.
> Help me to be all prayer and never to cease praying.
> > –A puritan Prayer[114]

Prayer is at the heart of the ministry of a chaplain, and it is the clear command of scripture. The Lord Jesus taught His disciples that "they ought always to pray, and not lose heart."[115] Not uncommonly, it is the only ministry that a chaplain may have in the throes of a crisis. Even those who are antagonistic toward religion very often appreciate the intercessory prayer of a godly minister. What chaplain has not heard the deep concern in the voice of someone experiencing trauma and then sensed the immediate relief when they call upon God for solace and strength? Prayer is the balm that sooths the disquieted spirit and turns the mind to the understanding that God is ever present. Proverbs 27:10 reminds us that in the day of calamity, "better is a neighbor who is near than a brother who is far away," because the one who is nearby can bring a needed reminder that "God is our refuge and strength, a very present help in trouble"[116] in the midst of the trauma. Often, the chaplain is the person who brings that reminder.

The chaplain must be devoted to the practice and provision of prayer, and exercise continual diligence in maintaining a vibrant prayer life. That is a significant challenge. Chaplains,

---

114   Arthur Bennett, ed, The Valley of Vision, A Collection of Puritan Prayers & Devotions, Carlisle, Pennsylvania, Banner of Truth Trust, 1994, 146

115   Luke 18:1

116   Psalm 46:1

by nature, are often people of action who quickly spring to the assistance of those in need. It is a winsome quality, but one that can easily interfere with the foundation of prayer. Ben Patterson, in his book *Deepening Your Conversation With God* expresses a frustration shared by many chaplains in noting the confession of a nineteenth century missionary, Mary Slessor, when he insisted: "Mary Slessor was right about prayer: 'Praying is harder work than doing ... but the dynamic lies that way to advance the kingdom.'"[117] It really is easier to do than to pray, but praying ought to be the first response of the first responder. That means that chaplains need to stay on praying ground, as the old saying goes.

The thought takes my mind back to the birth of my oldest son. At his ripe old age of twenty-one hours I was informed that there were serious problems with bleeding around the brain and they had not been able to stop it. The prognosis was grim and they had no words of encouragement for me. After praying with his Mother, I retired to our apartment to pray. It occurred to me that, perhaps, there might be some presumptuous sin of either omission or commission that might hinder my assault on the throne of grace, and so I began to pray that God would reveal it to me so that I might confess it. I was taken aback as my mind was filled with disturbing recollection of sins. One by one I wrote them on slips of paper, sought forgiveness and burned them on a plate. Into the evening I prayed until I could bring my Son before the Father with the conviction of a pure heart. Happily, the next day there was improvement and just a couple weeks later he was released from the hospital and I dedicated him to God with the same conviction with which I had recently confessed my sins. That lesson stands out to this very day as one of the most profound experiences of prayer I have ever known. It was a valuable lesson that impressed upon me in a striking way

---

117 Patterson, B., & Goetz, D. L. (1999). *Vol. 7: Deepening your conversation with God.* The pastor's soul series; Library of leadership development (17). Minneapolis, Minn.: Bethany House Publishers.

the importance of remaining up to date in prayer so that there will be no hindrance when a special need arises. Occasionally that experience comes to mind when given an opportunity to pray with someone who is facing the most difficult day of their life, perhaps the death of a child or a spouse, and it serves as a reminder to stay the course on prayer.

Public prayer, however, is a controversial topic. Those who oppose it often do so in the belief that it violates the separation of Church and State. On the other hand, those who are denied the opportunity to pray in public argue the free establishment clause. Thankfully, prayer, or at least the form of prayer, persists in the culture. Despite the considerable secularization of the American society and the vocal opposition of the religious and political left, it is still common for invocation and/or benediction to be offered at civic functions. There is little anyone can do to discourage private prayer, so it is not surprising, that it is chaplaincy and other venues of community ministry that are facing a concerted challenge to the practice, particularly in the public arena. There have been numerous lawsuits against the use of prayer in public life, much of which centers around the language of prayer, i.e. praying in Jesus' Name. The discomfort of those who are not familiar with prayer is often observed in their reference to its practice. It is not uncommon, for instance, for someone to call on the chaplain to say "a few words" as though simply inviting him to pray would be a religious statement that they or others might find offensive or at least uncomfortable. For the most part, the typical reticence to prayer is somewhat amusing, but there are some serious and disturbing challenges that must be addressed.

Objections to public prayer in the United States began to emerge in a big way in the middle of the twentieth century. Opponents were successful in manipulating activist courts to render several rulings prohibiting even voluntary prayer in schools and elsewhere in public life. Several attempts to enact legislation to clarify the issue failed. Primarily leftist and anti-

Christian factions kept the pressure on with numerous law suits intended to discourage prayer and, for that matter, any recognition of God in public, such as the display of the ten commandments or Christian symbols. Savoring their early victories they became bolder, demanding that "In God We Trust" be removed from our coins; the words "under God" be struck from the Pledge of Allegiance; the Ten Commandments be removed from public buildings; and nativity scenes and Christmas trees be banned from community property. Encouraged by the often inexplicable logic of activist judges and the generally lackadaisical response of a significant portion of the population, a flawed understanding of the separation of Church and State was transformed into a general perception of the separation of God and State. The result has been culturally, morally and spiritually debilitating.

Since chaplaincy functions largely in a civic setting, the controversy concerning public prayer is at the forefront of concern. Chaplains are expected to give careful thought to the language of prayer so as to avoid unnecessary exclusion. In the military, distinction is made between prayer that takes place in the context of worship or personal discourse and that of military formations where attendance is required. Civilian chaplains face similar concerns when called on to pray at a public function where attendance by people of other faiths or no faith are either required or expected to attend. In a culture where so many have been made sensitive to real or imagined slights to their beliefs, it is wise to consider the impact of the language of prayer. There is little that can be done to assuage those who object to any prayer at any time by anybody, but there are some who have sincere concerns, and chaplains should bear in mind that Christ died for them as well. There is nothing to be gained by deliberately causing offense, especially in a group setting where the opportunity to address any misconceptions is highly unlikely.

Increasingly, the controversy about prayer revolves around the common practice of Christian chaplains saying "in Jesus' name" at the beginning or end of a public prayer. More and more, it has become a litmus test for whether prayer is considered acceptable in a public or multi-faith setting, particularly among those who object to the Christian faith. Christians, on the other hand, are quick to point to scripture to establish that they must pray in the Name[118] of Jesus, because they are instructed to do so by the Lord Jesus Himself. Many Christian ministers view any restriction of their familiar format of prayer as a denial of their free exercise of religion. In view of this, any discourse on the role of a chaplain in public prayer must be thoughtfully considered. The burning question facing Christian chaplains is this: Must a Christian recite the words "in Jesus' name" (or a reasonable facsimile) for a prayer to be biblically acceptable?

Six times during the Passover feast (commonly known as the last supper) in John chapters fourteen through seventeen, the Lord Jesus makes reference to praying in His Name.

> Whatever you ask in my name, this I will do, that the Father may be glorified in the Son. If you ask me anything in my name, I will do it. John 14:13-14

> You did not choose me, but I chose you and appointed you that you should go and bear fruit and that your fruit should abide, so that whatever you ask the Father in my name, he may give it to you." John 15:16

> In that day you will ask nothing of me. Truly, truly, I say to you, whatever you ask of the Father in my name, he will give it to you. Until now you have

---

118　In an attempt to distinguish between praying in the Name of Jesus as a reference to His authority and simply reciting the words "in Jesus' name," the author has elected to capitalize the word "name" when the intention is to refer to Christ's authority, and not capitalize the word when referencing the mere recitation of the phrase. An exception to this rule is the quotations of scripture.

asked nothing in my name. Ask, and you will receive, that your joy may be full. "I have said these things to you in figures of speech. The hour is coming when I will no longer speak to you in figures of speech but will tell you plainly about the Father. In that day you will ask in my name, and I do not say to you that I will ask the Father on your behalf..." John 16:23-26

Furthermore, Ephesians 5:20 speaks of "giving thanks always and for everything to God the Father in the name of our Lord Jesus Christ..." James 5:14 makes reference to the Name of Jesus in regard to praying for the healing of the sick. James instructs us to "pray...in the name of the Lord."

There can be no doubt that the Lord Jesus desires that Christians pray in His Name. We must therefore ask what does it mean to pray in the *Name* of Jesus? The word used in all of the above cited references is ὀνόματί [onomati] from the root ὄνομα [onoma]. The word can refer to a name, a title, authority, power or status. Strong's Exhaustive Concordance of the Bible gives us additional insight: "The name is used for everything which the name covers, everything the thought or feeling of which is aroused in the mind by mentioning, hearing, remembering, the name, i.e. for one's rank, authority, interests, pleasure, command, excellences, deeds etc."[119] The definition of the word does not by itself provide the answer to the question, what does it mean to pray in the name of Jesus? It does; however, point to several interpretations that are more complex than mere recitation of the words "in Jesus' name." Since the Lord Jesus gets His name from the Father we might do well to examine how the name of God the Father is employed in scripture. A few examples should suffice.

The first such reference is found in Genesis 21:33: "Abraham planted a tamarisk tree in Beersheba and called there

---

119 Strong, J. (1996). *The exhaustive concordance of the Bible : Showing every word of the test of the common English version of the canonical books, and every occurrence of each word in regular order.* (electronic ed.) (G3686). Ontario: Woodside Bible Fellowship.

on the name of the LORD, the Everlasting God." Two names for God are employed here, LORD and the everlasting God; two of several names by which God is described in the Old Testament. A reasonable explanation would be that Abraham was petitioning God on the basis of both who and what He is, LORD (YHWH) and the everlasting God (El-Olam).

In Exodus 3:14-15, God made a remarkable statement about His own name: "God said to Moses, 'I AM WHO I AM.' And he said, 'Say this to the people of Israel, I AM has sent me to you.' God also said to Moses, 'Say this to the people of Israel, The LORD, the God of your fathers, the God of Abraham, the God of Isaac, and the God of Jacob, has sent me to you. This is my name forever, and thus I am to be remembered throughout all generations.'" This familiar passage holds great significance to both Jew and Christian with regard to the Name of God. When Moses queried God about who He was, God replied by simply stating that He was. It is the Hebrew word from which we get the English Jehovah, a name so revered that no Jew would pronounce it. In the very next verse, God went on to identify Himself as the God of Moses' fathers, the God of Abraham, the God Isaac and the God of Jacob and then He went on to insist "this is my name forever, and thus I am to be remembered throughout all generations." In this instance, at least, God's name was more than just a declaration of His identity; it was also a memorial, and one cannot escape the observation that He cited not one, but multiple names.

In Exodus chapter 34, God's name is employed to describe attributes of God. While Moses had been in the mountain receiving the Ten Commandments, the people of Israel had constructed an idol to worship God in a disobedient fashion. Upon the return of Moses, the tablets were destroyed and a great judgment came upon the people. A second time, Moses went to Sinai where God again inscribed new tables of stone. Exodus 34:5-7 records: "The LORD descended in the cloud and stood with him there, and *proclaimed the name of the* LORD. The LORD passed before him and proclaimed, 'The LORD, the LORD, a God merciful and gracious, slow to anger, and abounding in steadfast love and faithfulness, keeping steadfast love for thousands, forgiving iniquity and transgression and sin, but who will by no means clear the guilty, visiting the iniquity of the fathers on the children and the children's children, to the third and the fourth generation.'" (Italics mine) In this passage, God defined His name by reference to His attributes. Just a few verses later in Exodus 34:14 before He sent Moses back to the people, God reminded him "...for you shall worship no other god, for the LORD, whose name is Jealous, is a jealous God..." In this instance, His name is Jealous, yet another reference to His name citing His attributes.

Might the same be said of the name of Jesus? In chapter five of his general epistle, James is writing of the coming of the Lord. Three times in verses eight, nine and eleven James makes a clear reference to Jesus and names Him "Lord." It is reasonable, even imperative, that we understand the reference to "Lord" in verse ten as a fourth reference. James 5:10 says, "As an example...take the prophets who spoke in the name of the Lord." The prophets spoke in the "name of the Lord," but did they know Him as Jesus? By what name then did they prophesy? Does it not make perfect sense that they spoke through the *authority* of Christ, who though He had not yet been "found in human form,"[120] is equal with the Father?

In Acts 8:12, we find another example of scripture referencing, not the given name of Jesus, but the attributes that are implicitly understood by the Name of Jesus. "But when they believed Philip as he preached good news about the kingdom of God and the name of Jesus Christ, they were baptized..." It would be remarkable indeed if Philip found it necessary to convince the people of Samaria that belief in the mere given name of Jesus was unique. There is no indication that anyone

---

120 Philippians 2:8

questioned His given name. The debate was not over His name, but His authoritative claim to be the promised Messiah. They were saved and then baptized, because they received the message concerning the kingdom of God and believed that Jesus Christ is who He is, "the Lamb of God Who takes away the sin of the world!"[121] It was not the *recognition* of His given name that brought them to salvation, but the *submission* to His Name [attributes]. This passage stands in stark contrast to the account in Acts 5:40 concerning the opposition to the name of Jesus by the Jewish rulers. The council and the high priest in Jerusalem had forbidden the apostles to "speak in the name of Jesus"[122] They knew Jesus' name in the common sense, they even stated it, but they did not recognize His attributes or submit to His authority and they forbade the apostles to proclaim His attributes and authority to the people.

There is no doubt that there are New Testament references to the given name of Jesus and nothing more; and there are occurrences in the New Testament when the name of Jesus points to His authority and attributes. What, then, is the intention of the word when the Lord Jesus instructed His disciples to pray in His Name? If by that instruction He meant that they needed to say "in Jesus' name amen" at the end of their prayer, we strive in vain to find a New Testament example, for no prayer in the Bible contains that language.

When I was a young boy the family would gather around a large radio receiver in the living room and listen to radio dramas. Many of them were stories about the police and their efforts to bring criminals to justice. In the same way that today's television dramas, sitcoms and commercials introduce us to familiar statements that find their way into our daily language, the old radio shows popularized expressions that became well-known to nearly everyone. One such familiar saying can help us understand the meaning of praying in Jesus' name. In radio shows about law enforcement, the police would finally arrive at the home of

---

121   John 1:29
122   Acts 5:40

the criminal, knock on the door and declare: "Open in the name of the law." They identified themselves to make it abundantly clear that they had the authority to gain admittance. It was not the *word* "law" to which they appealed. It was the *authority* of the law that granted them the right to enter the premises. Likewise, it is evident that the mere words *"in Jesus name"* apart from the recognition of His attributes and authority cannot render a prayer valid or invalid. Believers have the right to approach God in prayer because of the death, burial and resurrection of Christ as a propitiatory sacrifice for sin and the repentant sinner's subsequent justification before God by faith. It is the authority by which they bring their petitions to God. No other appeal is worthy; no other appeal will touch the heart of God; no other appeal grants access to the ear of God; no other appeal enters into the will of God. Hebrews 11:6 makes that pretty clear in saying "without faith it is impossible to please him, for whoever would draw near to God must believe that he exists and that he rewards those who seek him." Others need not apply.

The Holy Spirit teaches us to pray, and even He intercedes according to the will of God. "Likewise the Spirit helps us in our weakness. For we do not know what to pray for as we ought, but the Spirit himself intercedes for us with groanings too deep for words. And he who searches hearts knows what is the mind of the Spirit, because the Spirit intercedes for the saints according to the will of God."[123] The emphasis and encouragement in prayer is on the attributes and will of God, not the language employed by those who petition Him. When a true Christian prays, he *is* praying in the Name of Jesus, for there is no other basis on which we may enter into fellowship with God in prayer. But because of the death, burial and resurrection of Christ as our redeemer, "we have an advocate with the Father, Jesus Christ the righteous."[124] That is the authority and assurance with which we may approach the throne of grace in confidence that our prayer will indeed be answered according to the will of God.

---

123   Romans 8:26-27
124   1 John 2:1

The reader should not interpret these remarks as a dissuasion of employing the phraseology "in Jesus' name" in prayer. It is entirely proper and permissible and even desirable. The point, rather, is that some evangelical and fundamental Christians are unnecessarily driven away from chaplain ministry because of the perception that they will not be allowed to pray "in Jesus' name," and even view it as somehow invalidating their prayer or as a betrayal of the Lord Jesus, if they do not employ that particular language. Since the meaning of praying in Jesus' Name is a biblical reference to the authority by which we pray, the Christian minister need not be overwhelmed by the suggestion that the common phraseology (dare I say mantra?) not be intoned in some circumstances. To pray in Jesus' Name means to pray on the basis of faith in the death, burial and resurrection of Christ by which one is granted access to the throne of grace where the believer has an advocate facing the Father – the Lord Jesus Christ.

In James 4:13–15 we find an admonition not unlike the encouragement to pray in Jesus Name. "Come now you who say, 'Today or tomorrow we will go into such and such a town and spend a year there and trade and make a profit' – yet you do not know what tomorrow will bring. ….Instead you ought to say, 'If the Lord wills, we will live and do this or that.'" On that basis of this verse, it is my habit to always qualify my intentions by stating something to the effect of "the Lord willing." It has some value in testimony to others to be sure, but am I to believe that if I fully understand the sovereignty of God in all the affairs of men, yet neglect to say "if the Lord wills," I am sinning? I think not. Neither have I in any way denied my Lord if I fail to say "in Jesus Name" in my prayer, though it is my regular practice to do so whenever appropriate.

The importance of this issue to chaplaincy is evident. Praying in Jesus' name has become a point of contention for those who foolishly want to eliminate prayer in the public arena. Many Christian chaplains feel that a denial of their desire to employ whatever language they wish in prayer is an abrogation of their free exercise of religion. Increasingly, the issue has proven to be divisive on both sides of the controversy. Prayer can pose a dilemma for chaplains. On the one hand, we have an overriding responsibility to remain faithful to God in how we pray; on the other, we are admonished to be understanding of the disparate views of those who have a different understanding of who He is, or who have little regard for Him. Is it possible to do both and remain faithful to our Lord? I believe it is if we understand that praying in Jesus' Name is more than the recitation of the phrase and rests more solidly in the authority by which we are granted access to the throne of grace. Given this understanding, it behooves us to give very careful attention to the practice of prayer, understanding that much of the time it may be the only ministry the chaplain will be able to provide.

Unfortunately, the matter of praying in Jesus' name has tended to put the focus on the rights of the chaplain instead of the needs of those to whom the chaplain ministers. That should never occur. An unfortunate example is the ill-advised demonstration by a United States Navy chaplain who initiated a hunger strike in front of the White House in a failed attempt to persuade the President to issue an Executive Order guaranteeing Christian military chaplains the right to "pray in Jesus' Name" while in uniform. After eighteen days, despite the fact that the President did not issue such an order and nothing changed, he declared victory. Much attention was given to the "rights" of chaplains; some members of Congress came to the protesting chaplain's defense; well-meaning political organizations raised lots of money; and those who oppose public prayer were able to say "I told you so."

Overlooked in the demonstration was the fact that there is no such prohibition. Military chaplains pray freely in uniform regularly in chapel services, in counseling sessions, in personal witness and elsewhere. Since chaplains are charged with ministering to everyone under their care, it is expected that they will not alienate them by employing language that is perceived by them to do so. The entire event was based on a misrepresentation of the issue. Military chaplains are not *forbidden* to pray in Jesus' Name while in uniform, and if in an isolated instance they are, it is a violation of military policy. They are cautioned about the use of exclusionary language only when praying at a formation or event when attendance is required and there is the expectation that there may be people present who might feel excluded by certain forms of sectarian prayer. This caution is not applied solely to Christian prayer, but clearly it is distinctively Christian prayer that draws the most objection. That is just a fact, not only in the military, but in every venue. While conducting a Christian chapel service or praying with someone one-on-one, and numerous other occasions, a chaplain is free to pray as he is led to pray within the bounds of common sense. If indeed, the instruction to pray in Jesus' Name is a reference to the authority by which we petition God, there is no biblical requirement that a particular phrase be recited to validate the prayer. That is in keeping with every example of prayer in the New Testament. It certainly is not objectionable to do so, but the chaplain should consider whether this perceived freedom falls under the category of becoming all things to all men that we might by all means save some[125] as outlined in the previous chapter.

It is of note that those who share the greatest and most knowledgeable concern for the continuation of chaplaincy in the armed forces expressed reservation with the proposition of employing a presidential order to guarantee the chaplain's right to pray as they see fit, rather than making an appeal to the Constitution. Leaders of the Military Chaplains Association of the USA (MCA) and of the National Conference on Ministry

---

125   1 Corinthians 9:19-23

to the Armed Forces (NCMAF), comprised of most of the military chaplain endorsers, expressed concerns about the issuance of a presidential order. [126] They were joined by the National Association of Evangelicals, who issued their own extensive statement on religious freedom for soldiers and military chaplains. Their concern, for the most part, was based on the realization that what is granted by presidential order can be taken away by a subsequent presidential order. On the basis of these current directives and the common practice of the various military chaplaincies, the then National President of the Military Chaplains Association (a fundamental evangelical Christian chaplain) expressed his concern with the call for the aforementioned presidential order in a letter to the President which said in part:

> At present there is a movement to gain your intervention through Executive Order regarding the rights of military chaplains. We certainly value the liberty of fellow citizens to seek this action. However, on the basis of argument thus far presented, we believe that such intervention is ill advised and unnecessary. Issues of religious free exercise and accommodation for any military personnel – including chaplains – can be properly resolved at this time within the existing authority of the Secretary of Defense."[127]

Since the chaplain's ministry is provided by Public Law consistent with the Constitution, it is unwise to seek redress from a less permanent and more political process. We must bear in mind that whatever freedoms we enjoy as Christian chaplains must also be granted to chaplains of other faiths. Must we then have a presidential order to guarantee Imams the right to pray in

---

126   To be fair, some military chaplain endorsers did support the demonstration and the desire for a presidential order.

127   Murdoch, John B., 2006, A letter to the President of the United States, January 19, 2006

the name of Allah (which would be objectionable to Christians and Jews); Roman Catholic Priests the right to pray in the name of Mary (which would be objectionable to Protestants, Baptists and Free churches); or Wiccans the right to pray in the name of the mother goddess (which would be objectionable to all of the above)? Bad idea!

Subsequent to the failed attempt at obtaining a presidential order, concerned members of Congress attached language to a defense-spending bill that sought to provide for prayer in Jesus' name at the discretion of the chaplain. The Associated Baptist Press reported that "the House Armed Services Committee attached the prayer amendment to a routine military appropriations bill on a party-line vote," stating that the chaplain "shall have the prerogative to pray according to the dictates of the chaplain's own conscience, except as must be limited by military necessity, with any such limitation being imposed in the least restrictive manner feasible."[128] On the surface, this appears to be a well worded and helpful solution and perhaps a better resolution than the presidential order approach. There are some important problems with either action; however, that should be a concern for evangelical and fundamental Christian chaplains.

The first of these is that this action has the potential to upset the balance that has worked so well for well over two hundred years in the United States armed forces. The guarantee of the free exercise of religion for everyone has been the foundation upon which military chaplaincy has been permitted. Chaplaincy in the United States military services has withstood several serious challenges over the years and has become a working model for the whole world. It is questionable whether legislation that surely will be seen to favor one religion over another can sustain the perception of fairness. Though the Senate did not concur with the House amendment in 2006, and it did not become law, similar motions are put forth annually. If

---

128   Associated Baptist Press, May 12. 2006, www.abpnews.com/1022. article

ever enacted into law we can expect legal challenges that may then subject chaplain's prayer to the whims of activist judges.

A second consideration is whether new legislative language is really necessary. Current military policy that has been in effect for many years, already guarantees the free exercise of religion for all members of the armed forces, including the chaplain. The 2003 iteration of Department of Defense Directive 1300.17 provides the following guidance which applies to all branches of military service.

> "A basic principle of our nation is free exercise of religion. The Department of Defense places a high value on the rights of members of the Armed Forces to observe the tenets of their respective religions. It is DoD policy that requests for accommodation of religious practices should be approved by commanders when accommodation will not have an adverse impact on military readiness, unit cohesion, standards, or discipline."[129]

The previously suggested legislative language is somewhat similar to that found in the Department of Defense Directive, but introduces a new consideration raising the question: When is it appropriate to determine that the conscience of a chaplain interferes with military necessity? Some have suggested that this provision, if adopted and taken to the extreme, could result in a new category of conscientious objectors within the military.

The Department of Defense term for those who are appointed as chaplains in the armed forces is Religious Ministry Professional (RMP). Once appointed, the RMP is designated as a chaplain. Department of Defense Instruction 1304.28 to which all chaplains must agree before they begin their military chaplain career says the following:

---

129 U.S. Department of Defense, Directive Number 1300.17, 2003

> "The RMP is willing to function in a pluralistic
> environment as defined in this Instruction and to
> support directly and indirectly the free exercise of
> religion by all members of the Military Services,
> their family members, and other persons authorized
> to be served by the military chaplaincies."[130]

The definition of a pluralistic environment in this DoD
Instruction is found in Enclosure 2.1.8 as follows: "Pluralistic
Environment. A descriptor of the military context of ministry.
A plurality of religious traditions exist side-by-side in the
military."[131]

This Department of Defense Instruction is descriptive
of what we have termed common pluralism which in itself
presents no opposition to Christianity or any other religious
faith. Enclosure 3.1.1 of the same DoD Instruction further
speaks to the expectations of chaplains and chaplain endorsers
at the outset of their commitment to provide chaplain services.

> Religious Organizations that choose to participate in
> the Military Chaplaincies recognize the chaplaincies
> of the Military Departments serve a religiously
> diverse population and that military commanders
> are required to provide comprehensive religious
> support to all authorized individuals within their
> areas of responsibility. Religious Organizations
> participating in the military chaplaincies therefore
> express willingness for their RMPs to perform their
> professional duties as Chaplains in cooperation with
> Chaplains from other religious traditions....[132]

---

130   U.S. Department of Defense, Instruction Number 1304.28, 2004
131   U.S. Department of Defense, Instruction Number 1304.28, Enclosure
2.1.8, 2004
132   U.S. Department of Defense, Instruction Number 1304.28, Enclosure
3.1.1, 2004

The point of citing these guidelines is that the language employed and utilized in military chaplaincy, if applied consistently, already provides for the free exercise of religion for chaplains, and all military chaplains and chaplain endorsing agencies have already agreed to them.

A third observation for consideration is whether the wording of a legislative action would require a definition of what constitutes protected prayer. The language of the resolution we cited would have applied to other faiths as well. Such an action has the potential to open a Pandora's Box and release all manner of protected speech. A radical Moslem Imam, for instance, might feel led to encourage hatred and even violence against the Jews during a prayer service, and then claim that since it was prayer, it was protected speech. If this wording were to become a part of public law, it would be only a matter of time before we would encounter many more conflicting ambiguities regarding prayer in the military.

Finally, a legislative approach to protecting Christian prayer, if passed, would utterly fail to achieve its objectives. It would surely open the door to legal challenges that could result in even more stringent restrictions on prayer than are currently extant. History has shown us that the often activist courts are unprepared and ill equipped to render wise decisions regarding spiritual matters. The end result could be that the very prayer that well-meaning lawmakers intend to protect could be redefined into irrelevancy. It is somewhat ironic that Christians would find it necessary to seek the authority of the State to pray in the authority given us by Christ Himself, Who is the Lord of all States. "For kingship belongs to the LORD, and he rules over the nations."[133]

Military chaplaincy is not the only ministry in the public view that faces a challenge from the anti-prayer bunch. Police chaplaincies, jail ministries, hospital chaplaincies and even workplace chaplains are increasingly confronted with

---

133 Psalm 22:28

this opposition, but often without the protections afforded to military chaplains. The regrettable truth is that those who would restrict the way that Christians pray are usually very protective of their own religious rights, hence their objection to the name of Jesus. There is little concern on the part of the complainants that Christians are offended by the use of Christ's name in profanity, but the intoning of His name in prayer wakens a pathetic sense of sensitivity. It's hard to ascribe sincere motives to that kind of interference with the free exercise of religion. Often they are advocates of freedom *from* religion in the guise of freedom *of* religion. It is important that Christian chaplains not employ that same disingenuous spirit in retaliation. "For though we walk in the flesh, we are not waging war according to the flesh. For the weapons of our warfare are not of the flesh but have divine power to destroy strongholds. We destroy arguments and every lofty opinion raised against the knowledge of God, and take every thought captive to obey Christ,..."[134] We ought rather to be expectant of the opposition and remain faithful to our calling and to the stewardship of the glory of God in the realization of 1 Peter 4:14–16, "If you are insulted for the name of Christ, you are blessed, because the Spirit of glory and of God rests upon you. But let none of you suffer as a murderer or a thief or an evildoer or as a meddler. Yet if anyone suffers as a Christian, let him not be ashamed, but let him glorify God in that name."

The emphasis on the *rights* of the chaplain is a disturbing trend in our religious culture. Chaplaincy is not about the chaplain. It's about the people the chaplain serves and most importantly, about the glory of God. When the media attention is on the chaplain's rights, the ministry of chaplaincy suffers and, more tragically, so does the testimony of God's grace. Our Lord Jesus Himself reminded us of this in Matthew 20:27-28, "... whoever would be first among you must be your slave, even as the Son of Man came not to be served but to serve, and to give his life as a ransom for many."

---

134 2 Corinthians 10:3-5

Upon appointment as a chaplain, a clergyman voluntarily surrenders a degree of autonomy in exchange for the opportunity to minister, an agreement that is too often overlooked or misunderstood. The military chaplain takes on the dual role of chaplain and military officer. As a chaplain, under current directives, he is responsible to his endorser for accountability as a minister. As an officer, he is responsible to the military chain of command. It is not so different in civilian chaplaincies associated with civic agencies in which the chaplain is responsible to the agency for his duties and accountable to the church for his ministry. There is a duality that calls for a measure of subordination that is somewhat unfamiliar in a church setting. In exchange for this additional commitment, the chaplain is granted privileged ministerial access to individuals and information not readily available to others. The willingness and ability of the chaplain to minister cordially to people of all faiths or of no faith is a key factor in the granting of those privileges. There are several practical steps that chaplains can take to maximize their opportunities for prayer while minimizing unnecessary squabbles that tend to hinder their ministry.

The first of these is to *give careful thought to the occasion of prayer*. God has an interest in everything we are doing. Our prayer should reference that attention in specific ways. Most people appreciate God's interest in their endeavors. When there is a military change of command, for instance, it would be proper to seek God's wisdom and provision for the incoming commander, and offer thanks for the efforts of the outgoing commander. Since it is a required formation, it is not appropriate to offer what would be considered an overtly sectarian prayer. The same is true of a civic function when a chaplain is called upon to lead an invocation and/or benediction. Chaplains should understand the difference between a voluntary and mandatory gathering, or in the context of civic functions the difference between a religious and secular gathering. More liberty is granted the military chaplain when conducting a voluntary field worship service than when participating in a Commander's Call or other required formations. What may be considered poor judgment at a staff meeting may be perfectly acceptable when leading in worship or praying with an individual. In any venue, it is important that chaplains get to know the people that they serve and understand their religious views and sensitivities. If ministry is the goal, it makes no sense to deliberately offend someone. Romans 12:18 teaches us, "If possible, so far as it depends on you, live peacefully with all."

Preparation produces powerful public prayer. In pastoral ministry, I was reluctant to write a prayer in advance, but as a chaplain, I have learned the wisdom of preparing my prayer for a public function. Writing a prayer can help the chaplain to express a proper reverence for God and recognition of His Sovereignty while avoiding inadvertent slips of the tongue that may have repercussions in the context of official functions. Sometimes it is not possible or practical. There is, after all, the tongue in cheek proverb that insists that the chaplain must always be ready to preach, pray or die without notice. Most of the time giving thought to the purpose of the function; understanding who will be present and planning language that honors God and to which the gathering can relate; and compiling appropriate thoughts will pay dividends. *Acknowledge only the truth*. Chaplains are never required to say or pray something that they don't believe to be true. Give careful thought to expressing the truth in a clear and non-threatening way, but do not succumb to the temptation to merely mouth meaningless platitudes. Avoiding unnecessary controversy does not mean that we have to adopt error. *Always acknowledge the dominion and Providence of God*. Chaplains are expected to represent the presence and interest of God. Make it a point to refer to His sovereignty in every prayer. Phrases like "we acknowledge Your oversight in the affairs of men and nations;" or "we thank You for the leaders that You have set in place;" bear testimony of God's greatness in a non-denominational way. Quote brief statements from the Bible that reveal the person of God, but *avoid the temptation to preach in prayer*. A secular civic occasion is hardly the place to rehash lasts Sunday's sermon, but a thoughtful and meaningful prayer may lead to an opportunity to witness one-on-one at a later time, or even encourage a listener to visit your church or chapel services. *Keep it short and simple*. Public prayer is not the place to showcase your theological vocabulary of seventy-five cent words. By the same token, just quoting shallow platitudes is equally inane. Maintain a balance that is meaningful and appropriate to the attendees.

Another brief clarification with regard to praying in Jesus' Name is appropriate here. Though some Christian chaplains feel that they *must* repeat the phrase with every prayer, there is no New Testament example. To pray in Jesus' Name means to pray on the basis of our union with Christ secured through saving faith, which gives us the right to come to God in prayer. Much of the time the chaplain is free to say whatever he is led to say, but in civic functions or military formations where attendance is not optional, it is wise to avoid language that may be considered offensive by some. There is little to be gained and a great deal to lose if we persist in fighting an unnecessary battle. Rather than make it a divisive issue, we ought to expend our energy on communicating the glories of God in a way that opens the door for future discussion. When a chaplain prays at a public function in a manner that acknowledges the sovereignty of God and is considerate of the sensitivities of those who are present, the opponents of public prayer are deprived of resources in their opposition. In addition, if they object it will be apparent that their real hostility is not only to Christian prayer, but to the acknowledgment of God in our culture. There may be meaningful opportunity for subsequent one-on-one ministry with the participants in such gatherings as a result of the chaplain's consideration.

Finally, *it may be necessary on occasion to just say "No"* to an invitation to pray. There are times when the purpose or activity of a function is such that you just cannot lend your presence to it. If a chaplain is uncomfortable with it, there is no shame in declining to pray. That, too, can be a testimony that speaks more loudly than attempting to accommodate a function or activity that cannot be encouraged without compromising doctrine or principle.

CHAPTER SEVEN

THE CHAPLAIN AND PROSELYTISM

Few words have evoked more passion on the part of chaplains of all flavors than *proselytize*. There are those who fear the influence that chaplains of other faiths may have on their flock, and see a restriction on proselytizing as a safeguard. For the most part, fundamental and evangelical chaplains are strongly committed to a biblical view that mandates that they evangelize and they are suspicious, to say the least, of any desire to limit their outreach. Others are persuaded that it really doesn't matter, because they find validity in whatever faith someone espouses. Another group decries any kind of spiritual influence and sees proselytizing as an unwelcome attempt to force them to confront religion. Since chaplaincy often requires some form of cooperation between clergy of disparate religious understanding, it is essential to chaplaincy that there be some sort of adaptation to provide for them to relate to one another and to those to whom each of them minister.

Occasionally, a chaplaincy will be comprised entirely of ministers who profess the same faith, but even then it is likely to include denominations representing differing views within the broader spectrum of their faith group. In a professed Christian chaplaincy, for instance, you may find Arminians and Calvinists; fundamentalists, evangelicals, neo-evangelicals and neo-orthodox; traditionalists and revisionists; liturgical and relaxed; reformed and dispensational; premillenial, amillenial and postmillenial; men and women; baptists and pedo-baptists; sprinklers and immersionists; separatists and inclusivists; social drinkers and tee-totalers; theologians and students. In some respects there is more to divide us than to unite us in chaplaincy. Since chaplaincies are not typically identified by denomination, to whatever degree necessary, chaplains must give serious thought to pluralism even within their own professed faith group. The burning question for many is this: Can a bible-believing Christian minister be involved in chaplaincy in which proselytism is forbidden?

The restrictions on proselytizing are, in the view of the author, a much more daunting challenge to the evangelical chaplain than the issues of pluralism and praying in Jesus Name. It is sometimes understood as a direct assault on the chaplain's ability to evangelize in obedience to the imperative command of scripture. Christian ministers are "ambassadors for Christ"[135] and are therefore responsible to represent the interest of the Savior in a fallen world. Praying for His disciples in John chapter seventeen, our Lord Jesus made reference to this ministry saying, "As you sent me into the world, so I have sent them into the world."[136] Every Christian minister is familiar with the marching orders of the Church issued by Christ Himself: "…you will receive power when the Holy Spirit has come upon you, and you will be my witnesses in Jerusalem and in all Judea and Samaria, and to the end of the earth."[137] The exclamation of every obedient minister of Christ to the unsaved is "We implore you on behalf of Christ, be reconciled to God."[138]   Holy Scripture is clear in asserting that the reconciliation we espouse is only available through the Lord Jesus Christ for "…there is salvation in no one else, for there is no other name under heaven given among men by which we must be saved."[139] For the obedient bible-believing Christian, evangelism is an inescapable responsibility. Some would then insist that it is incompatible to any Christian endeavor to embrace a ministry that discourages proselytism.

---

135   2 Corinthians 5:20
136   John 17:18
137   Acts 1:8
138   2 Corinthians 5:20
139   Acts 4:12

In the marketplace of religious ideas, proselytism has become a concept that must be faced and understood by Christian chaplains. Like pluralism; however, it has a multitude of definitions and applications. Several religious communions find value in all non-exclusive religions and have no particular compulsion to persuade anyone of anything. Some are content to merely hold on to what they have and feel no duty to reach out to others. Even some who profess Christianity are somewhat disinterested in evangelism. On the other end of the spectrum are cults that are aggressive in the expansion of their influence to the point of deception and even violence. Though it has become politically incorrect to reference it, the example found in many countries controlled by the followers of Islam is a testimony of proselytism gone wild. At some point on the scale even evangelical Christians would find proselytizing abhorrent. In a free society people are able to embrace whatever religious convictions they wish and in the exercise of that same freedom, they are able to express those convictions to others. The restraint of one is no different than the suppression of the other.

Much of the objection to so called proselytizing does not focus on the sharing of conflicting religious ideas so much as on sacred expression that is considered exclusive in its teaching as opposed to inclusive or pluralistic. Carson distinguishes these three viewpoints thusly:

"Briefly, exclusivism is the view that only those who place their faith in the Christ of the Bible are saved; inclusivism is the view that all who are saved are saved on account of the person and work of Jesus Christ, but that conscious faith in Jesus Christ is not absolutely necessary: some may be saved by him who have never heard of him, for they may respond positively to the light they have received. And pluralism is the view that all religions have the same moral and spiritual value, and offer the same potential for achieving salvation, however 'salvation' be construed."[140]

It is not uncommon for a chaplaincy to contain adherents of all three of the above referenced beliefs. Among denominations and religions that view themselves as only one of many valid measures of spiritual enlightenment, there seems to be an almost uniting tolerance. The emergence of radical pluralism has encouraged, even mandated, forums to share divergent religious ideals. Biblical Christianity with its exclusivist insistence on the uniqueness of God and faith in the redemptive sacrifice of Jesus Christ as the only means of salvation is conceived as a threat to that balance. The Bible rejects any notion of inclusivism and; therefore, the ire expressed by those who most strongly object to proselytizing is directed largely toward Christianity, Christian ministers and Christian institutions in an attempt, in their view, to level the playing field. It should not come as a surprise to any informed bible-believer.

On the surface, the discouragement and even outright prohibition of proselytizing would indeed discourage Christian ministers from engaging in chaplaincy, except for the realization that proselytism and evangelism are not synonymous. In fact, the dichotomy between proselytizing and evangelism is made evident in chaplaincy. For example, the Code of Ethics for the United States Army Chaplain Service states that "I will not proselytize from other religious bodies, but I retain the right to evangelize those who are non-affiliated." The United States Air Force Code of Ethics contains an almost identical statement: "I will not actively proselytize from other religious bodies. However, I retain the right to instruct and/or evangelize those who are not affiliated." In the wake of these long accepted positions, a law suit was filed against the United States Air Force on October 31, 2005 by one Michael L. Weinstein *et al* which specifically referenced the statement on proselytizing and charged the Air Force with

---

140   Carson, The Gagging of God, 278

violation of First Amendment guarantees of the right to freedom of religion. The suit alleges an informal policy of "evangelizing, proselytizing and otherwise actively challenging the religions of its members" at the Air Force Academy. Apparently, in citing both *evangelizing* and *proselytizing*, even those who apply the most restrictive understanding of proselytizing make a distinction between the two.

The Air Force responded with a revised guideline for the free exercise of religion on February 9, 2006 which stated: "Nothing in this guidance should be understood to limit the substance of voluntary discussions of religion, or the exercise of free speech, where it is reasonably clear that the discussions are personal, not official, and they can be reasonably free of the potential for, or appearance of, coercion." The Air Force guidelines that were adopted after careful consideration and the participation of chaplains of disparate faith groups clearly implies that the intent of the prohibition of proselytizing is to discourage religious discourse that is involuntary, understood to be an official affirmation on the part of government, or in any way coerced. Biblical evangelism is none of those. Evangelism, to be effective, must of necessity be voluntary. It certainly does not represent the official mandate of the government, nor should it, and a coerced conversion is totally contrary to biblical Christianity. This understanding is completely compatible with the Baptist distinctive (also accepted by many others) of individual soul liberty.[141]

Christian chaplains need not be intimidated by concerns about proselytizing so long as they conduct the sharing of their faith in a non-coercive one-on-one basis or within the framework of defined religious services. It may sometimes

---

141   The Baptist distinctive of Individual Soul Liberty is that every individual is granted by God the liberty to choose what his conscience or soul dictates is right, free from the coercion of human institutions, be they civil or religious. Every soul is responsible to God for his or her own beliefs and actions, and must not be forced to hold to a religious faith or tenet against his will. Baptists (and others) believe that this competency is a gift from God and; therefore, human beings are not simply puppets to be manipulated.

be true in civilian chaplaincies that constraints that are more restrictive are placed on the chaplain, but these restrictions are not the norm. Some hospitals, for instance, may forbid their chaplains to discuss anything based on their own belief system instead of the belief system of the patient. These limitations are often mitigated simply by obtaining permission to share Christian truth before proceeding. The process outlined in First Peter 3:15–16 is a wise example: "...in your hearts honor Christ the Lord as holy, always being prepared to make a defense to anyone who asks you for a reason for the hope that is in you; yet do it with gentleness and respect, having a good conscience, so that, when you are slandered, those who revile your good behavior in Christ may be put to shame."

The effective Christian chaplain must become adept at obtaining permission to share his faith in considerate evangelism. Forcing his views upon someone or insisting that they are mandated by public or workplace policy introduces the element of coercion and crosses the line to what would then correctly be considered proselytizing – a practice that is almost universally prohibited in chaplaincy. Understanding the difference between evangelism and proselytizing will free the chaplain to seek opportunity for witness as the Spirit of God opens the understanding of the recipient to the truth of God. Without that work of God, no amount of coercion or persuasion will bring any person to Christ. Our Lord Jesus Himself insisted, "No one can come to me unless the Father who sent me draws him. And I will raise him up on the last day."[142]

Unfortunately, there has been reluctance on the part of some evangelical ministers to participate in chaplaincy in the mistaken belief that the mandates concerning proselytizing and praying in Jesus' name would require them to compromise their convictions. It is true that public policy insists that a minister who functions as a chaplain is expected to be considerate of those who espouse differing religious and social views. Nothing

---

142 John 6:44

in that expectation; however, is contrary to what is expected of us as Christian ministers committed to the proclamation of the Gospel of Jesus Christ. Why would we not want to be loving and considerate in our association with all people? Second Corinthians 5:14 reminds us that it is the love of God that constrains us to witness. Romans 13:10 insists that "Love does no wrong to a neighbor; therefore love is the fulfilling of the law." Ephesians 4:15 describes maturity in Christ as "speaking the truth in love," which is perfectly in keeping with the benediction of Paul in First Thessalonians 3:12: "...may the Lord make you increase and abound in love for one another and for all, as we do for you." To rule out chaplain ministry on the basis of restrictions on proselytism would in fact diminish witness (evangelism) as an expression of the unfailing love of Christ. The greater concern ought to be that Christian chaplains not abandon witness under the guise that it violates the prohibition of proselytism.

Many years ago in my first pastorate I was privileged to have in my congregation some dear folk who were formerly from the Plymouth Brethren fellowship. We had some differences on matters of church polity, but we had much in common and enjoyed a mutual love for the Word of God. The oldest member of the family was a retired minister who shared with me stories of the beloved Plymouth Brethren preacher and Bible teacher, Harry Ironside. One such story has stuck in my mind through all my years of ministry. It seems that Dr. Ironside was addressing a group of Plymouth Brethren at a gathering at which several Baptists were present. At the conclusion, the Brethren folks gathered around Ironside to ask questions and fellowship with him. One them queried: "Dr. Ironside, I'm curious as to why you didn't take advantage of the opportunity to set the Baptists straight on church polity." Ironside's reply, I'm told, was: "I was afraid they might ask to see a working example." Throughout this examination of Christian chaplaincy, I have endeavored to provide biblical examples of New Testament ministry. As we conclude our discussion of the three "P"s (*pluralism, prayer* and *proselytism*), one more New Testament illustration is warranted — a working example.

The Apostle Paul provides us with this working example of ministry in the kind of pluralistic environment in which chaplains are expected to function. It is also an instance of ministry in the secular arena where chaplains serve. Paul came to Athens after being sent away from Berea where he had enjoyed a short, but fruitful ministry. Those who were stalking him from Thessalonica had come and stirred up the people against the preaching of the Word. It was not unlike the hostility that today's Christians might expect to encounter from radical pluralists. (The opposition that Paul faced was consistent with the hostility found of the Council in Jerusalem that had forbidden Peter and John to speak or teach in the name of Jesus.[143] It is of note that Peter and John responded with obedience to God and continued to evangelize.[144]) While Paul waited in Athens for Timothy and Silas to join him, he was able to take advantage of an opportunity to present Christ to the advisory council of Athens, known as the Areopagus. These were the men who supervised the education, ethical, cultural and religious matters in Athens. Present were Stoics who were the pantheists of their day who believed that everything was governed by fate. Also present were Epicurians who denied God's providence and sovereignty over the world. Their primary interest was pleasure and they believed that there was nothing after death. It was a pluralistic crowd and a challenge for any chaplain. The biblical account will provide us with additional insight on ministry in our own time:

> Now while Paul was waiting for them at Athens, his spirit was provoked within him as he saw that the city was full of idols. [17] So he reasoned in the synagogue with the Jews and the devout persons, and in the marketplace every day with those who

143 Acts 4:18
144 Acts 4:19-20

happened to be there. **18** Some of the Epicurean and Stoic philosophers also conversed with him. And some said, "What does this babbler wish to say?" Others said, "He seems to be a preacher of foreign divinities"—because he was preaching Jesus and the resurrection. **19** And they took him and brought him to the Areopagus, saying, "May we know what this new teaching is that you are presenting? **20** For you bring some strange things to our ears. We wish to know therefore what these things mean." **21**Now all the Athenians and the foreigners who lived there would spend their time in nothing except telling or hearing something new.

22 So Paul, standing in the midst of the Areopagus, said: "Men of Athens, I perceive that in every way you are very religious. **23** For as I passed along and observed the objects of your worship, I found also an altar with this inscription, 'To the unknown god.' What therefore you worship as unknown, this I proclaim to you. **24** The God who made the world and everything in it, being Lord of heaven and earth, does not live in temples made by man, **25** nor is he served by human hands, as though he needed anything, since he himself gives to all mankind life and breath and everything. **26** And he made from one man every nation of mankind to live on all the face of the earth, having determined allotted periods and the boundaries of their dwelling place, **27** that they should seek God, in the hope that they might feel their way toward him and find him. Yet he is actually not far from each one of us, **28** for "'In him we live and move and have our being'; as even some of your own poets have said," 'For we are indeed his offspring.' **29** Being then God's offspring, we ought not to think that the divine being is like gold or silver or stone, an image formed by the art and imagination of man. [30] The times of ignorance God overlooked, but now he commands all people everywhere to repent, [31] because he has fixed a day on which he will judge the world in righteousness by a man whom he has appointed; and of this he has given assurance to all by raising him from the dead."

[32] Now when they heard of the resurrection of the dead, some mocked. But others said, "We will hear you again about this." [33] So Paul went out from their midst. [34] But some men joined him and believed, among whom also were Dionysius the Areopagite and a woman named Damaris and others with them. Acts 17:16-34

Of first interest in relation to a contemplation of witness in a hostile environment is the remarkable opportunity itself. How did Paul come to the attention of the authorities and then gain the prospect of sharing his faith with them? The answer to that question can help us develop a strategy for evangelism in a public arena that prohibits proselytism.

Paul was provoked by sin. Verse sixteen says that "his spirit was provoked within him as he saw the city was full of idols." The word *provoked* is παρωξὐνετο (paroxyneto), from παροξὐνω (paroxyno). It means to be upset, angered, irritated or distressed. It is a passive verb, which tells us that the idolatry Paul observed was acting upon his spirit to provoke him. He was bothered by sin; distressed by it; driven to ministry. How refreshing. It is not unusual in our day for chaplains to grow hardened to the sin about them. Ministry in the public venue exposes one to all manner of debauchery and tragedy. It's easy to grow cold and cynical and withdraw into the perceived safety of indifference. The frequency and proximity of sin can harden the conscience and the constant pressure to avoid offense can lead to the acceptance of all manner of disorderly behavior. It is sometimes difficult for chaplains to sustain pure speech in an environment where profanity is rife and off-color jokes are the staple. This is particularly true in law enforcement and fire chaplaincies. Chaplains need to be constantly reminded of the admonition of Colossians 4:6: "Let your speech always be gracious, seasoned with salt, so that you may know how you ought to answer each person." It is often the practice in our modern culture to withhold judgment and criticism of a fallen society. Even many churches are careful to avoid biblical criticism of certain popular or protected life styles and sexual orientations for fear of repercussion, choosing rather to dish out shallow sermonettes for christianettes that cannot offend but will seldom produce true repentance. It is a refreshing thing when a minister is provoked by sin and is thereby driven to ministry.

Paul was persistent in his testimony. Verse seventeen informs us that the result of Paul's angst over the idolatry of the city was that he "reasoned in the synagogue with the Jews and the devout persons, and in the marketplace every day with those that happened to be there." It is of note that his disputation was the result of the provocation occasioned by his exposure to the prevailing sin of the city. He did not ignore it, or excuse it, or justify it, or simply wash his hands of it. Had he done any of those things, he would have had no testimony to the Athenians and they would, no doubt, have taken his silence for approval. Furthermore, he would not have been given the opportunity to address the Aeropagus. Instead, Paul confronted it as he had opportunity to do so.

He disputed [διελεγετο – dielegeto] a word that is sometimes translated *to make a speech*. That means that he spoke out, but the scope of his testimony indicates that he did so in a manner that caught the attention of a great number of people. He was not content to simply register his disdain; he set out to persuade them of the truth whenever they were open to his evidence. Matthew Henry makes an interesting observation about Paul's witness in Athens:

"He did not, as Witsius observes, in the heat of his zeal break into the temples, pull down their images, demolish their altars, or fly in the face of their priests; nor did he run about the streets crying, "You are all the bond-slaves of the devil," though it was too true; but he observed decorum, and kept himself within due bounds, doing that only which became a prudent man. 1. He *went to the synagogue of the Jews,* who, though enemies to Christianity, were free from idolatry, and joined with them in that among them which was good, and took the opportunity given him there of disputing for Christ, v. 17. He discoursed *with the Jews,* reasoned fairly with them, and put it to them what reason they could give why, since they expected the Messiah, they would not receive Jesus. There he met with the devout persons that had forsaken the idol temples, but rested in the Jews' synagogue, and he talked with these to lead them on to the Christian church, to which the Jews' synagogue was but as a porch. 2. He entered into conversation with all that came in his way about matters of religion: *In the market—en teμ agora,* in the exchange, or place of commerce, *he disputed daily,* as he had occasion, *with those that met with him,* or that he happened to fall into company with, that were heathen, and never came to the Jews' synagogue. The zealous advocates for the cause of Christ will be ready to plead it in all companies, as occasion offers. The ministers of Christ must not think it enough to speak a good word for Christ once a week, but should be daily speaking honourably of him to such as meet with them."[145]

Paul demonstrated a compassionate and consistent strategy that commends itself to the ministry of a chaplain. He was successful

145   Henry, Matthew. (1996, c1991). *Matthew Henry's commentary on the whole Bible : Complete and unabridged in one volume* (Ac 17:16). Peabody: Hendrickson.

in gaining a hearing because he was sincere and consistent in his testimony.

Paul was persecuted for his witness. We must not overlook the reality of criticism. They called Paul a "babbler" in verse eighteen. It was not a very nice appellation. The Greek word [σπερμολόγος – spermologos] is a combination of two words, one meaning *to collect or gather* and the other meaning *a seed*. Literally, *a seed picker*. It was used of one who picked up and passed on insignificant things. In Athens, it often referred to people of little social value who collected garbage and sold it in the market place. It would have been a term of contempt; something akin to someone today who rummages through garbage cans to find bottles to sell at the recyclers.

In spite of the ridicule, Paul persisted in his testimony of Jesus and His resurrection. Ultimately, his perseverance paid off and, as a result, he was given a remarkable opportunity to witness. It should come as no surprise to a chaplain that he must be prepared for ridicule and worse if he is faithful to his calling. We are to expect it. The Lord Jesus, in the Sermon on the Mount, warned of such treatment: "Blessed are you when others revile you and persecute you and utter all kinds of evil against you falsely on my account."[146] Another time He said "…you will be hated by all for my name's sake"[147] "Indeed, all who desire to live a godly life in Christ Jesus will be persecuted.…"[148]

There is a prevailing push in chaplaincy to gain acceptance, which often stifles testimony, but the Christian chaplain must remain faithful as a steward of the Gospel of Jesus Christ if his ministry is to produce spiritually fruitful opportunity. The chaplain will do well to remember the admonition of Paul in Ephesians 6:11–13:

Put on the whole armor of God, that you may be able to stand against the schemes of the devil. [12]

146 Matthew 5:11
147 Mark 13:13
148 2 Timothy 3:12

For we do not wrestle against flesh and blood, but against the rulers, against the authorities, against the cosmic powers over this present darkness, against the spiritual forces of evil in the heavenly places. [13] Therefore take up the whole armor of God, that you may be able to withstand in the evil day, and having done all, to stand firm.

Paul was preaching the Gospel. In the latter part of verse eighteen, we find a clue as to why Paul was being ridiculed and why he subsequently was invited to address the civic leaders. "...because he was preaching Jesus and the resurrection." The Christian chaplain must always be reminded that it is the proclamation of the Gospel that offers deliverance to the weary soul. It is fine to understand the nuances of the agency served and relate to the experiences of the soldier, police officer, fireman, prisoner, or civil servant, but ultimately it is for the Gospel and the Word of God that the chaplain is on the scene. Crisis response is the daily duty of a Christian chaplain, but the goal is the Gospel. The ministry of presence has as its aspiration the exposure of the scriptures and the application of its truth in the life of those who are served by chaplaincy. If all they require is an encouraging presence during and following trauma, or a referral to the services of a psychiatrist, or a confirmation of their physical homeostasis, a crisis response worker will suffice. It is competent proclamation and appropriate application of the Word of God to the situation at hand and the life of those who are served that distinguish Christian chaplains from all other encouragers. "So faith comes from hearing, and hearing through the word of Christ."[149] Crises and chaplains come and go, but as Peter so eloquently stated, "... the word of the Lord remains forever. And this word is the good news that was preached to you."[150]

Preaching the Gospel brings both blessing and curse. Often, chaplains grow discouraged when their ministry seems

---

149   Romans 10:17
150   1 Peter 1:25

fruitless and rejection of the Word is commonplace, but it is as much a part of God's plan to put forth the Gospel when it is rejected as when it is embraced. 2 Corinthians 2:15, 16 provides us with valuable insight: "For we are the aroma of Christ to God among those who are being saved and among those who are perishing, to one a fragrance from death to death, to the other a fragrance from life to life...." The majority will not come to Christ through the efforts of the chaplain, but the timely proclamation of the truth about the death, burial and resurrection of Jesus Christ as the only sacrifice that can satisfy the justice of God is also an essential message when it is scorned. The righteousness and the wrath of God is revealed in the Gospel so that those who reject it "are without excuse."[151] It is a solemn responsibility and as much a Gospel ministry as it is when the response is favorable.

Paul was preaching (ευηγγελιζετο - euengelizeto). The word means to tell the good news. There is an element of joy in the meaning. Most godly preaching does not emanate from a pulpit, but from the proclamation by life and lip of a devoted servant of God who has found his greatest joy in Jesus Christ. The Holy Spirit employs a derivative of the word in Luke 2:10 to describe the announcement by the angels of the birth of Christ: "...Behold, I bring you *good news* of great joy..." (Italics mine) It was commonly used to announce a victory. Paul's focus was on the good news or Gospel, and Christ's victory over sin and death. The middle voice of the verb tells us that the Gospel was acting upon Paul and he was entered into the results of that action. He could not be the same since surrender to the Savior; his life was changed forever and he could do nothing less than to express that testimony of joy to the Athenians at every opportunity. Christian chaplains must not lose sight of that message, nor their commitment to announce it. As they said in the Ford commercials, it is job number one. Paul's faithfulness to the Gospel message reminds us of the wisdom

---

151 Romans 1:17-20

of Proverbs 22:29,   "Do you see a man skillful in his work? He will stand before kings; he will not stand before obscure men." The Aeropagites were not kings, but they were prominent men in a highly pluralistic community that had no interest in proselytism, and yet they were drawn to a godly witness.

Thus far we have considered the testimony that led to the opportunity to bring the Gospel to the public arena. There are several important observations about how Paul then ministered in that culture. Ministry in a church usually presupposes some familiarity with the Bible and the tenants of the Christian faith. In that context, there is general agreement on the major issues of biblical teaching. In our modern culture, it is seldom the case in the public sector. Often, chaplains are called upon to minister in a completely pagan setting, or at least in a venue where there is no prior knowledge of Christian truth, and to do so in the throes of a crisis. That was pretty much the situation in Athens. The philosophers of that great Greek city were biblically ignorant and faced a spiritual crisis of which they had no inkling. Into that arena, Paul is called upon to minister.

Paul employed a principle of pedagogy taking them from a known to a related unknown. In other words, he took them from where they were to where they needed to go. He did not just stride onto their porch and begin to move the furniture. Often, Paul would begin with a familiar Old Testament truth as a starting point to expound a related principle. Examples of this are found in Romans chapter 7 where he spoke to those who understood the law; First Corinthians chapter 9 where he began with Moses to explain his ministry to Jew and Gentile alike; and the book of Galatians where he employed their understanding of Jewish circumcision to point them to their liberty in Christ. But these Athenians knew little of Moses or of Christ or of the traditions of the Jews, so he made an effort to understand their orientation. He didn't just walk by and criticize their error, he looked for some common reference that he could employ to point them to Christ. Then he led them away from their perception of a pantheistic god to the revelation of the transcendent God of creation. He took them from the veneration of an unknown god to a vision of the true and living God Who is sovereign over all. He guided them from the poetic concept of their own imagination to the paradisiacal conclusion that God had after all ordained their steps.

It is little different from the wise practice of a missionary who surveys his intended field and then devises a strategy for evangelization. Too often, we encounter pluralistic restrictions on proselytizing and throw up our hands in despair. Better to do what we routinely do in missions; devise a sensitive and respectful approach that gains permission to "make a defense to anyone who asks you for a reason for the hope that is in you; yet do it with gentleness and respect, having a good conscience..."[152]

Despite the ridicule heaped upon him, Paul approached the Athenians with courtesy and respect. He found some common ground upon which he could direct their attention to the true God, but he was careful not to agree with or accept their doctrinal error. His approach was not to incorporate their pagan understanding into a tacit acceptance of Christ as has periodically been true of some who profess Christianity.[153] He did not embrace their error and find a way to sanctify it with Christian application. He did not overlook their error and treat it as insignificant. He did not look for a seeker-friendly way to bring God down to their level and make Him more acceptable to them. He did not shrink from the concepts of repentance and judgment, as suggested by some evangelicals. He did; however, approach them with sensitivity and carefully explained the claims of Christ beginning with what little common ground he could find. Ultimately, Paul called them to repentance and warned them of the judgment that is to come. Some believed and most did not, but he was a faithful steward of the message

152 1 Peter 3:15

153 I refer here to historical instances where pagan practices have simply been incorporated into Christian practice and celebration.

of the Word of God; a savor of life to some and a savor of death to others.[154]

Chaplains need not be deterred from ministry by man-made perceptions regarding pluralism, prayer or proselytism. If Christian chaplains are divinely called, adequately prepared and properly associated with a local church they will be able, in the strength of Christ, to meet the challenges of a pagan culture and enjoy a rewarding and constructive ministry for the glory of God.

---

154 2 Corinthians 2:15-16

CHAPTER EIGHT

ONE FINAL DEFINITION

In the introduction to this writing we drew the readers attention to two very important words, *Christian* and *biblical*. Throughout the following chapters we referenced the term *biblical Christian*, or *biblical Christianity*. This was not done with a view toward throwing down a gauntlet or in any way demeaning others. It is rather a sensitivity to the obvious realization of a diverse denominational and doctrinal understanding of what constitutes Christianity. There are some who may equate Christianity with citizenship in a predominantly Christian country, or birth into a family in which the parents espouse a Christian belief. Some religious expressions are historically considered cults by most Christians yet represent themselves as Christian communions. Even within the familiar denominations, there are fundamentalists, evangelicals, neo-orthodox, emergent, and what have you. There are those (such as the author) who hold the Bible to be the inerrant, infallible, verbally inspired Word of God and the only rule of faith and practice for Christians. There are those who believe the Bible to be simply a classic book of religious stories. Some see it as but one witness alongside of and equal to tradition or other writings. Others hold the Bible in esteem, but question the veracity of its recorded miracles and authorship. And there are some who select for themselves the portions to which they ascribe. And yet, all of these may insist that they are Christians and most would be included in the mix identified as Christian chaplains. So, the reader can readily see that some definition is useful.

Historically, Christianity is defined, at least among Bible believers, by five fundamental tenets: (1) The Deity of Jesus Christ, the Son of God and God the Son; (2) the virgin birth of Christ; (3) the death of Christ as a vicarious blood atonement for sin to satisfy the righteous justice of God; (4) the bodily resurrection of Christ from the dead; and (5) the inerrancy of the Bible. Some would add to these *fundamentals* the personal bodily return of Christ to the earth. This certainly is not the entirety of what Christians believe, but these cardinal doctrines define what has been often referenced as "the historic Christian faith." Though the distinctions have blurred somewhat over the years, historically, those who hold to these fundamentals were and are called fundamentalists.

Perhaps the best way to define what is intended by the term *biblical Christianity* is to lay out the biblical Gospel, for this understanding constitutes the core of Christian truth. It begins with a Creator God who does all things for His glory. The first man, Adam, sinned against God in a deliberate act of disobedience and hence sin has passed upon all for "all have sinned and fall short of the glory of God."[155] "Therefore, just as sin came into the world through one man [Adam], and death through sin, and so death spread to all men because all sinned... "[156] Should anyone posit the unlikely deception that they are without sin, scripture makes it clear that all are already guilty by virtue of their identification in Adam. Hence, all are not only guilty through individual acts of sin, but even before that, all are born in sin. This condition is terminal resulting in death, both physical and spiritual. Sin is the root cause of death, destruction and depravity both for the individual and for all human society. God's human creation is thereby found to be incapable, in itself, of enjoying a right relationship with God.

If this was the entire truth, we would be left with profound depression, but the good news (Gospel) is this: Though man is incapable of obtaining forgiveness of sin

---

155 Romans 3:23
156 Romans 5:12

on his own, God has intervened to purchase for Himself a redeemed multitude. This redemption (literally a purchase in the marketplace) requires that the sentence of death for sin be carried out. "For the wages of sin is death, but the free gift of God is eternal life in Jesus Christ our Lord."[157] This justice is necessary to satisfy the righteousness of God Who is in every way incompatible with sin. "...God is light, and in him is no darkness at all. If we say that we have fellowship with him while we walk in darkness, we lie and do not practice the truth."[158] A suitable blood sacrifice is required to satisfy the demands of righteousness, for "...under the law almost everything is purified with blood, and without the shedding of blood there is no forgiveness of sins."[159]

God's plan was to provide Himself a sacrifice in the person of Jesus Christ, Who is the Son of God and God the Son. "In the beginning was the Word, and the Word was with God, and the Word was God. ... And the Word became flesh and dwelt among us, and we have seen his glory, glory as of the only Son from the Father, full of grace and truth."[160] The Lord Jesus entered into His creation through a virgin birth thus avoiding the sin nature from Adam. He lived a righteous life totally without sin and; therefore, He was qualified on both counts to offer Himself as an acceptable sacrifice for the sins of the world. His death on a cross was purposeful, according to God's plan before the foundation of the world. "...this Jesus, [was] delivered up according to the definite plan and foreknowledge of God ..."[161] His death was vicarious (on our behalf) and propitiatory (it satisfied God's justice). "For our sake he made him to be sin who knew no sin, so that in him we might become the righteousness of God."[162] This atoning sacrifice was God's

---

157 Romans 6:23
158 1 John 1:5, 6
159 Hebrews 9:22
160 John 1:1, 14
161 Acts 2:23
162 2 Corinthians 5:21

gift of love. "For God so loved the world, that he gave his only Son, that whoever believes in him should not perish but have eternal life."[163]

Unique to Christianity is the understanding that following the crucifixion of Christ, He was placed in a guarded tomb and on the third day, He rose from the dead and appeared in bodily form to hundreds of witnesses. Scripture teaches us, "...he was delivered up for our trespasses and raised for our justification."[164] The Resurrection of Christ is at the heart of Christian belief. So much so that the Apostle Paul insisted, "... if Christ has not been raised, then our preaching is in vain and your faith is in vain."[165] The Bible goes on to say, "But in fact Christ has been raised from the dead, ...For as in Adam all die, so also in Christ shall all be made alive."[166]

Up to this point, the large majority of those who profess Christianity are in agreement, at least in general terms. That which distinguishes fundamental Christianity from every other religious perception hinges on the understanding that salvation (forgiveness of sins, justification before God, a new nature, eternal life, Heaven) is a gift from God and is granted solely on the basis of faith. "For by grace you have been saved through faith. And this is not your own doing; it is the gift of God not a result of works, so that no one may boast."[167] All other religion seeks either the forbearance or appeasement of God through the accumulation of deeds and actions that are perceived to be pleasing to God, a view that is sometimes shared even by some who profess Christianity. The Bible reminds us that since we are all sinners, we are already under condemnation. "...one trespass led to condemnation for all men..."[168] "For all have sinned and fall short of the glory of God..."[169] This condition renders us

---

163 John 3:16
164 Romans 4:25
165 1 Corinthians 15:14
166 1 Corinthians 15:20 & 22
167 Ephesians 2:8, 9
168 Romans 5:18
169 Romans 3:23

incapable of pleasing God through any amount of good works or of any human action, because, as the Bible states it, we are "condemned already."[170] But happily, the Lord Jesus, speaking specifically of salvation, reminded His disciples, "What is impossible for men is possible with God."[171]

The glorious Christian truth and assurance is that "Salvation belongs to the LORD!"[172] It is the free gift of God; therefore, it cannot be earned or purchased by any work of man. It is attainable only by faith alone in the work of Christ when He offered Himself on a cross to satisfy the justice of God on our behalf. It is granted by the grace of God. Grace is the favor of God given to those who have earned His wrath. "The wages of sin is death, but the free gift of God is eternal life in Christ Jesus our Lord." Grace is given. Our works receive a wage. That wage is death. Grace negates the appeal of good works. "But if it is by grace, it is no longer on the basis of works; otherwise grace would no longer be grace."[173] How then is one to receive this gift? The Bible is clear on that important question. "'The word is near you, in your mouth and in your heart'[174] (that is, the word of faith that we proclaim); because, if you confess with your mouth that Jesus is Lord and believe in your heart that God raised him from the dead, you will be saved. For with the heart one believes and is justified, and with the mouth one confesses and is saved."[175] There is not a word of human goodness or achievement in that declaration; therefore, we conclude that salvation is by faith alone in Christ alone. It is a serious insult to God to suggest that the death of Christ must be supplemented by our own deeds or piety. Adding our works to the work of Christ by insisting that we must yet earn our salvation is nothing less than saying to God His sacrifice is not sufficient to save us

---

170 John 3:18
171 Luke 18:27
172 Jonah 2:9
173 Romans 11:6
174 A quote from Deuteronomy 30:14
175 Romans 10:8-10

and; therefore, we must add to His redemptive work if it is to be complete. Such an idea is a sacrilege.

The faith of which we speak is no mere intellectual assent; it is a deep-seated trust in the redemptive work of Jesus Christ in His death, burial and resurrection. Meaningful faith will be manifest in two ways. The first of these is repentance, which means to change the mind. The child of God will experience a sorrow for and confession of sin, as he views these things in a new light. "Or do you presume on the riches of his kindness and forbearance and patience, not knowing that God's kindness is meant to lead you to repentance?"[176] "For godly grief produces a repentance that leads to salvation without regret, whereas worldly grief produces death."[177] The second evidence of true faith is the emergence of a new nature. "Therefore if anyone is in Christ, he is a new creation. The old has passed away; behold, the new has come. All this is from God, who through Christ reconciled us to himself..."[178]

One more brief word of clarification, for I would not leave the reader with the mistaken impression that good works are entirely without value. To be sure, we are not saved *by* works, but we are indeed saved *to* good works. "For we are his workmanship, created in Christ Jesus for good works, which God prepared beforehand that we should walk in them."[179] The point is not to eschew or denigrate good works, but to understand that they are of no value in obtaining salvation. "Now to the one who works, his wages are not counted as a gift but as his due. And to the one who does not work but trusts him who justifies the ungodly, his faith is counted as righteousness..."[180] The clear imperative of what we have termed biblical Christianity is this: "Believe in the Lord Jesus Christ, and you will be saved...,"[181]

---

176 Romans 2:4
177 2 Corinthians 7:10
178 2 Corinthians 5:17, 18
179 Ephesians 2:10
180 Romans 4:4, 5
181 Acts 16:31

for "there is salvation in no one else, for there is no other name under heaven given among men by which we must be saved."[182]

Dear reader, I plead with you to carefully search the scriptures and examine the insights shared in this book. They are intended to stimulate dialogue and evaluation of the ministry of chaplaincy. We bring our thoughts to a close as we began, remembering the folks in Berea who were commended as more noble than some others because "they received the word with all eagerness, examining the Scriptures daily to see if these things were so." As a result, "many of them believed."[183] Christian chaplaincy is a noble calling and careful consideration of biblical example and admonition can add much to its progress. May it please God to use it to His glory.

182 Acts 4:12
183 Acts 17:11, 12

Dr. Whit Woodard brings to print a wealth of insight into Christian chaplaincy. Having ministered as a missionary, pastor, and chaplain, he offers biblical and practical considerations that will stimulate the thinking of the reader. As a law enforcement chaplain, Whit has extensive experience as chaplain, Training Officer, Deputy Senior Chaplain and Administrator in a large multi-agency chaplaincy; and subsequent additional ministry as Senior Chaplain for a municipal police department.

In 2001, the International Conference of Police Chaplains recognized Whit as a Master Chaplain. In the military realm, he has twenty-five years experience as a chaplain in the United States Air Force Auxiliary, Civil Air Patrol. He began his chaplaincy career in CAP as a unit chaplain while a missionary pastor in California. In 2002, Chaplain Woodard was awarded the prestigious Distinguished Service Award by the Military Chaplains Association of the USA, and subsequently served as a member of the National Executive Committee.

In 2008, Woodard was named Chief of Chaplains for CAP, in which capacity he manages the largest all-volunteer chaplaincy in the world. As an Air Force Auxiliary chaplain, Woodard has also

provided extended chaplain ministry in the field for U.S. Army Active Reserve units and is a force multiplier for the Air Force Chaplain Corps. He has been cited for his support role in Operation Enduring Freedom. Dr. Woodard is a Trained Trainer in Critical Incident Stress Management for *Pastoral Crisis Intervention* and *Assisting Individuals in Crisis.* He has served four churches as pastor and as General Secretary of a council of churches.

His educational accomplishments include a Bachelor of Arts in Biblical Studies, Master of Divinity and Doctor of Ministry degrees.